The Classrooms of Miss Ellen Frankfort Confessions of a Private School Teacher

THE
CLASSROOMS OF
MISS ELLEN
FRANKFORT

CONFESSIONS
OF A
PRIVATE
SCHOOL TEACHER

By
Ellen Frankfort

Prentice-Hall, Inc.
Englewood Cliffs
New Jersey

The Classrooms of Miss Ellen Frankfort:
Confessions of a Private School Teacher
by Ellen Frankfort

© 1970 by Ellen Frankfort

Library of Congress Catalog Card Number: 75-101255

Printed in the United States of America • T
13-136200-3
Prentice-Hall International, Inc., London
Prentice-Hall of Australia, Pty. Ltd., Sydney
Prentice-Hall of Canada, Ltd., Toronto
Prentice-Hall of India Private Ltd., New Delhi
Prentice-Hall of Japan, Inc., Tokyo

TO MY PARENTS, MY FIRST TEACHERS

·°⧽ CONTENTS ⧼°·

·❦{THE YESHIVA}❦·

THERE ARE MANY ways of coming upon a career. Some people, like saints, are summoned from above while others, like doctors, are driven by mothers whose ambitions for their sons are said to fall just short of heavenly callings. As for myself, it was more a matter of stumbling.

I had, in fact, fulfilled all the family expectations by going to a good college, getting a good education, and graduating totally unprepared for anything. Four years of philosophy, in which I majored, had given me a training so universal that the only thing for which I could qualify was the further study of philosophy. Of course, this was no surprise. Has there ever been an employment ad in the entire history of *The New York Times* which began "Lady Philosophers Wanted"?

Earlier in the year there had been warnings of what awaited young women who turned away from academe without sufficient training. In the Spring, before graduation, the president of my college gathered together the recipients of fellowships for a cozy chat. There was, she observed, a pattern about this time each year which started with a general panic about getting married, led to a particular man, and culminated in the kitchen, which offered a temporary sanctuary for those seeking an escape from the self. But it was only temporary, she stressed, pausing to give those of us who were planning just such escapes a moment for thought. And I took the time to pray that I would be given the opportunity to flee from myself in the near future. The president was a very earnest lady. She had light blue eyes unadorned by glasses in front or circles below, and a face whose chief qualities were those of a Cape Cod shingle—sturdy, natural, and proper to the setting. None of us doubted one word she said. For her eyes, her face, her very being did not allow for doubt. It was, of course, for this reason that we could not take her seriously. We knew that the sincere and sensible lady talking to us had never experienced the need to prove herself as a woman; worrying just was not her style. Her gender had been assigned at birth, and to spend further time fussing about it would have struck her as unproductive.

The only reason we listened at all was because, in addition to running a college, she ran a home which included a husband and five children, which was exactly what most of us aspired to do. We knew we could pass any test intellectually, but could we become a wife? Could we mother a child? Could we manage a household? Those were the real tests.

And so we ignored the president's advice to go on with our education, but listened carefully as she confessed that she had not thought about marriage until she fell in love (and that took place at age 33). How comforting it was to hear that we could go through a dozen years of mistakes and emotional messes and still have time to settle down. As for fellowships, I personally felt enormous relief at having turned one down, and the president's chat did nothing to change my feeling, mainly because she seemed a species so different from myself that I could not imagine her understanding my needs of the moment. (It was rumored that her own daughter had left college to go into analysis, where she hoped to find out why she had always functioned so efficiently, and had suggested that her mother do the same—an idea roughly akin to having the Pope enter analysis in order to learn how to enjoy pornography without feeling guilt.)

Anyway, my graduation was several years ago, and the world was a more limited one. If I were graduating from college today I do not think I would be so concerned with security and stability. We may have been freer than our dear college president, but most of us still considered respectability respectable. We were a transitional generation in many ways; the offbeat was somewhat suspect, although the old fogey was on his way out. Kookiness was yet to be institutionalized; most of us looked like young Ivy League graduates as did the men we wanted to marry. I tell you all these things so you can appreciate the predicament a bright young female without a fiancé or good office skills faced upon graduation. Please remember, there was no Peace Corps, no Job Corps, no Vista or Volunteer Corps. The only marches recorded during four years of college were those to the altar.

The shocking revelations in the 1950's were that not everyone in a split-level suburb was happy and that men in gray flannel suits did not always feel fulfilled. I think my whole generation accepted compromise as one accepts the "given" in a geometry problem. The purity and authenticity demanded by the young today did not exist even as ideas.

And yet there were problems, even with imperfection as a

goal. For what were we to do? In our favor were our brains, but working against us were our numbers—a veritable army of bright young things all seeking a rest from school and some money (at least enough to support ourselves and our faithful cats).

Given these goals, there were few choices. One was publishing for English majors or advertising for ex-English majors who had leaped out of literature when forced to tackle Middle English. In either case you had to sacrifice a summer to learn speedwriting and stenography and other office skills. Then, in accordance with good medieval guild practice as taught in History 201, you could start out as an apprentice. If you showed some industry during the week and spent your weekends shopping for chic basic blacks, you might just qualify to join the respectable hordes of Ivy League women who each year genteelly storm the publishing "houses," most of which are located in large indistinguishable buildings.

If, for some reason, you didn't want to do anything as straight as that, there was another possibility. You could present yourself at a municipal building that even with only one literature course you would immediately identify as "Kafkaesque," where you would encounter endless forms, bent folding chairs, and sour clerks who told you it was not your turn even if you were merely asking for the ladies' room. The atmosphere was authentically grubby—the closest thing to today's antipoverty work.

It was here, in this big building, that you could become an investigator for the Department of Welfare. The appeal was to those who were uncomfortable with regularity and who liked being clumped with creeps, losers, and occasionally some of the most exciting characters around, who formed the prototype for today's community organizers. They were people who loved their clients, hated their paper work, and knew that they could leave whenever they wanted to without a sense of having disappointed a boss, for everyone agreed that the boss, municipal government, was his enemy as well as the enemy of the people it was trying to help.

It was at the Welfare Department that you saw Vassar girls having their first affairs with blacks; village chicks, who having already had their initiation rites, were now working to pay for their analysis where they were trying to discover what went wrong when. It was not a job for those with delicate sensibilities. But they were already neatly established in offices with lots of intelligent people like themselves doing dull work with the hope that one day they would use their intelligence.

By temperament I was somewhere in between the rebellious and the regular. Had I taken a course in sociology or read David Reisman I would have known the exact label for what I was. All I knew was that I did not want a nine-to-five routine, nor did I want to wander around tenements investigating people, making sure that they were not hiding some little luxury like a comb which their budget did not allow for that month.

It was by this kind of elimination that I came to consider teaching as a possible career, only to learn that it is not true that those who cannot do, teach. That is, not without first taking education courses or getting advanced degrees. And only one thing was worse than spending a summer learning speedwriting and that was spending a summer taking "Ed" courses. So I did neither and instead spent the summer in the sun wondering what I would do when the warm weather passed.

As I waited and sunned, I remembered my own elementary school. It was right across the street from where I lived. Early each morning at 8:00 o'clock I used to watch the teachers arrive before I reached that magical age when I too could start going to school. First Miss Beggs would arrive, with her little crown hat from which a long pheasant feather flew out at an angle. She was always accompanied by squat Miss Topper, who occasionally would carry a plant which had proven its durability in her own home before she took it to her classroom, which, in memory, seemed like a second home for both Miss Beggs and Miss Topper.

Miss Barret would drive up in her trim black car three minutes later, needing less time to arrange her hair since no hat had flattened it. She quickly parked in her usual spot. Sometimes Miss Beggs and Miss Topper would wait for Miss Barrett if they saw her car pulling up, and then all three would mount the white steps of the main entrance used only by teachers and latecomers and pass under the columns into the building, each fussing about who should hold the door open for the other two.

Then I would watch the children arrive. At first their noise made only a vague stir but as the numbers increased the noise rose to a crescendo and then was cut completely by a long, loud bell. Everyone stopped what he was doing and lined up. The latecomers ran fast toward the school in order to arrive before the side doors were locked. Once that happened, the only way to enter was through the main entrance, beyond which was a double wrought iron spiral staircase leading directly to the principal's office.

Weekends were strangely quiet in the school yard until the warm weather, when I would be awakened by the sound of a bat hitting a ball as the baseball players started the day, earlier each Sunday as summer approached. I knew summer had arrived when the first Good Humor ice cream truck sounded its bell for the baseball players in the school yard.

Living across the street from the school gave me other ways of keeping up with the seasons. The windows on the second and third floor, which housed the lower grades, were covered with pastel drawings depicting the various holidays. The first would go up for Halloween: wonderful witches with black wily cats humped across fences, followed in November by turkeys and pumpkin pies. Of course the school went crazy at Christmas time and even the fourth- and fifth-floor windows were filled with Santa Clauses, candles, and choir boys, all of whom suddenly disappeared in January, when all windows were washed. Now purified from the previous year, the windows were ready for February and cherry pies. I can't recall what went up for Lincoln's Birthday, but I now suspect that he was born too close to Valentine's Day and was passed over in favor of frillier commemorations.

By the end of my summer of sunning, my coat of tan made me feel armored to face the employment situation and in the autumn I picked up a paper to see what was available. Things had not changed much; there was no call for philosophers, all the interesting sounding jobs required good typing, and not even the Welfare Department had immediate openings. In desperation I called my college placement office, where I was informed of a part-time job that was just offbeat enough to interest me—teaching English in a Hasidic high school.

Now it turns out, you don't have to be Jewish to teach at a Yeshiva. As a matter of fact, it is a little better if you are not. That is, there's less chance of getting things wrong if you know nothing. Leave the Hebrew studies to those who know best— old Talmudic scholars with deep-set eyes, sad faces, and complexions made sallow from too little sunlight. And they, in turn, will leave the English studies to those less spiritually inclined.

But I knew none of this when I applied for the job as English teacher in the only all-girls' Hasidic high school in America. I had been told only two things by the lady who informed me of the job—that it paid very poorly and that the head rabbi was fanatically strict about sex. Now neither was exactly a come-on, but then as we've seen, I was not the most valuable commodity on the job market and could hardly be choosy.

The Yeshiva was located in a virgin slum of Brooklyn yet to be penetrated by urban renewalists, anti-urban renewalists, and others. To get to the Jewish section, I had to pass through the heart of gangland territory belonging to blacks (then known as Negroes) and Puerto Ricans, whose boundaries shifted with battle victories. When I got off the elevated train, the record store below was blasting Spanish music. Teenage boys were hanging around the pizza-ice cream store, hands in pockets, swinging back and forth on the heels of their shoes, while their girlfriends stood nearby in front of the pawn-broker shop in the shadow of its open iron gates, looking less cool and laughing more hysterically.

Within this setting was a neutral little strip of land belong-ing to the Orthodox Jews, unchanged, it seemed, from the time they had arrived. This part of the slum was crowded with bearded men in long black coats and wide-brimmed hats. Behind them walked peasantlike women who held the hands of their little long-haired boys as they hurried along amidst the neighborhood wars frequently fought by Puerto Ricans and blacks, who seemed to recognize the frailty of the Orthodox Jews and let them go on their way. The only link connecting all three ghettos was the mammoth bridge which brought the trucks into the area, creating an atmosphere of constant motion as they indiscriminately crossed the ethnic lines.

It still amazes me that the Jews were not more frightened than they seemed to be, living in such a violent setting. Now, in retrospect, I think I understand why they were left alone. They were as poor as their neighbors and with as few prospects for getting rich. The Jews did not own any large clothing stores; in fact, there did not seem to be one central shopping avenue. The Hasidic Jews did not own real estate; like their poor neighbors they rented their stores and instead of com-muting to better areas at closing time they often went to the rooms right in back of where they worked. The Hasidic Jews had to work near their homes so that they could observe the Sabbath laws and the many other carefully enforced restrictions in their daily lives. Above all, the schools were not any better than those the blacks and Puerto Ricans attended. In fact, they looked worse. Most were housed in condemned public schools built around the turn of the century, probably the only time that Jews have taken over what blacks and Puerto Ricans have abandoned.

"God alive, I must be lost," I muttered to myself.

"What's that Miss, God's alive?"

"No, no, no. I am lost and it has nothing to do with God."

"What are you looking for?"

"The Hasidic School for Girls."

"You can't be. Not if you have nothing to do with God."

"Huh?"

"I'm only kidding. My name is Anthony Canelli, and I can escort you right to the school. Don't worry, I'm not going to rape you. Just come with me. You've got to have faith if you're going to teach the Hasidic. I know, because I teach there myself."

"What did you say your name was?"

"Anthony Canelli, but call me Canelli. Most people do. Why are you eyeing me that way? I can see you don't believe me. Look, will it help if I put on my yarmulke? Wee bonnet, as a visiting Scotsman called it. Usually I wait until I get to the school. Here on the street it feels a bit funny."

"What do you mean?"

"Well you don't think Anthony Canelli is a Hasid, do you?"

"Frankly, Anthony Canelli doesn't even sound Reform Jewish to me."

"I'm not."

The Yeshiva itself was, as a student with poetic strivings put it, the color of caked blood. And the description was not only accurate but also significant, since Orthodox women spend one-fourth of their adult lives going to ritual baths to cleanse themselves of their monthly flow.

Inside, I almost tripped on the warped steps which slanted backwards.

"Ellen," said Canelli, "let's get down to some practical advice. Make out as if you oppose any literature that has to do with man-woman things."

"You mean oppose *all* literature? After all, even Shakespeare deals with man-woman things, as you put it."

"Right. So oppose Shakespeare, and oppose *Junior Scholastic,* which the girls are forbidden to read."

"What's left?"

"Don't worry about that now. Just oppose, oppose. Especially anything Rabbi Slutsky calls 'modern,' which will be at least fifty years old."

"Anything else?"

"Don't fail to bargain about salaries or Rabbi Slutsky will conclude you're dumb."

"I heard the salaries are so low, it hardly matters."

"Precisely. It's the principle of the thing."

"Where are you going?"

"Down for a quick knish. Want one?"

"I had better not. Suppose Rabbi Slutsky comes back?"

"Eating is considered a sign of wisdom here, Ellen."

"Still, I think I'll wait and save the knish for later."

Despite the decrepit atmosphere, a general air of gaiety prevailed. I gathered it was lunch time as the smell of grease arose from the basement, and I gathered Rabbi Slutsky did not remember the precise time of our appointment when I saw his cubicle, crowded with everything but him. (One had to gather things, for most of the people I heard talking spoke a broken refugee English.)

While I waited, I watched the girls running about in the hall, chasing each other. They looked healthy and robust, and it was hard to imagine that shortly, upon marriage, their heads would be shorn of hair and covered by kerchiefs and knitted hats, like those of the women I passed in the streets, leaving the features no place to hide. Why, I wondered, would any woman want to make herself so unattractive? I did not know that the reason was a very practical one—so that other men would not desire her and interfere with her familial fidelities. (A sociologist has it on record that there was only one known case of infidelity in this entire Hasidic community since World War II and then only one of the infidels was a Hasid.) If you want your wife to yourself do not make her into a showpiece. Of course; it makes perfect sense—and shortly I became accustomed to this coupling of the spiritual and the practical.

The only person in the office was a bearded man poring over some files, and he did not seem to take note of my presence, as if conditioned by the plain-looking women in his world not to recognize a member of the opposite sex when he saw one. Of course it was perfectly possible that he did not see me, so I decided to perch upon a large desk top. But I failed to notice that the space for the typewriter was vacant, and into it I fell.

"*Oy, gevalt,* did someone go breaking his noodle? Dvorah, *nu?* Are you all right?"

When Dvorah did not answer, a man came flying into the room. The first thing I noticed was his red beard, a wild and wooly affair, which I thought a bit inappropriate for a gentle and long-suffering scholar.

"So what do you want?" the man asked when I stood up.

"I would like to speak to Rabbi Slutsky."

"Speaking."

With the blunt reply came a conversion. Rabbi Slutsky, the gentle long-suffering scholar turned into Rabbi Slutsky, the fiery prophet. The interview began amidst old books piled everywhere.

"Pull that chair over, Miss, Miss, Miss—what's your name?"

"Frankfort," I told him as I began to remove some books from a bridge chair.

"Ignore the books," he said. "They're just here until the Fire Department leaves me alone. After they inspect, thank God, the books go back to the rear stairway where they belong. Because I want to make trouble, Miss Frankfort? No. . . . Because there is no library. So just remove the books and sit down a little."

I looked for a clear spot and finally placed the books in a wastepaper basket.

"Tell me, Miss Frankfort, what is your opinion of modern literature?"

"Shocking," I answered without hesitation. "As a matter of fact, I think it should be banned." And then I sat back to wonder if I had protested too much.

"Exactly so. When can we start work?"

"Uh, tomorrow, I suppose."

"Something's wrong with today?"

"Uh, no. Not really. But I think I would like a chance to prepare."

"What's to prepare in English? You speak the language. Right? You show the girls a little grammar one day. Maybe you have them write something. So what's to prepare?"

"Well, still, I did not count on starting today and would. . . ."

"So okay. Start tomorrow. Another day without English they will live too."

"What time do English studies begin?"

"When Hebrew studies end. Except we give our girls a little rest in between. So say be here at about three to three-thirty."

"And how long do English studies last?"

" 'Til five, except of course on Friday. On Friday we have no English studies."

"Then there are only four afternoons?"

"Right, just four afternoons and one hour Sunday mornings. Where else could you get such a deal?"

"Sunday mornings? Oh, Rabbi Slutsky. I'm afraid that I can't work on Sunday mornings."

"What's wrong with Sunday mornings?"

"Well, Sunday is a sort of . . . family day. You know, a time for close ties. The only day we can be together."

"*Oy, gevalt.* Every day is a family day, *nu?* You don't work on Sundays, you don't get paid, you know."

"I'll have to sacrifice that hour's pay, I'm afraid."

"Vat? An hour? It's one whole day less. Just that Sunday is a smaller day."

"How about half a day less, Rabbi Slutsky?"

"We'll make a bargain, four-fifths of a day less but that's all."

"It's a deal. See you tomorrow at about three to three-thirty."

"You're getting a bargain, so you should come at about three."

The next day I arrived at the school early, hoping to get to my class ahead of time so I could have a look around. But all the rooms were being used for Hebrew studies and I had no place to go. Rabbi Levy's office, the only other alternative, was already overflowing with books and I found myself hanging about the halls, trying not to lean upon anything with full force since so many structures looked ready to collapse of their own aged weight.

After waiting about fifteen minutes, I became aware that something extraordinary was being prepared. A voice yelled out from Rabbi Slutsky's room, "Read the list. Everyone here should please read the list."

Those instructions were followed by another set: "No. Don't read the list. Not until it's up." The second set seemed to make more sense. More screams.

"Who has a thumbtack?" Some girls who had been standing in the hall ran in to ask if there was any way to help.

"Scram," Rabbi Slutsky, who had now joined us, answered, raising a hand in good paternal fashion if they were not fast enough.

Now a new command. "Okay, everyone. Here's the list."
Was I everyone? Or were there others hiding inside between
old books, in wastepaper baskets, under Rabbi Slutsky's desk?
I watched gratefully as others began to arrive. One young-
looking man appeared, motorcycle helmet in hand, still clutch-
ing the keys as he reached the second floor.

"What's going on?" he demanded.

"*Buon giorno,* Canelli, is someone getting married?"

"Hold your horses, Adam, while I straighten my yarmulke."

Canelli turned to me, raised his eyebrows toward the make-
shift sign, "The List," and shook his shoulders. Gesturing is
contagious, and I shook my shoulders back. In front of us
both was a yellow piece of scrap paper with each teacher's
name typed on it. Next to each name was a day of the week.
I reread it. Canelli again looked at me and I again shook my
shoulders and nodded my head. Then Canelli pointed to the
top of the list; FIRE DRILL SCHEDULE was written in
large capital letters. I was still puzzled, so Canelli started a
conversation with words.

"Remember the Chicago fire where all those kids got
killed?"

I nodded.

"Well after that, the New York Fire Department paid the
Yeshivas a visit. Most of them are not in the very best of condition, shall we say." This last phrase he uttered with a small
laugh, pointing down at the warped floors. "Well, when they
arrived here, they learned from Rabbi Slutsky that not once
in the history of the school had there been a fire drill. And,
of course, as Rabbi Slutsky explained, there was good reason

for that. For you see, the iron stairs in back are used as book shelves since there is no space for a library. Naturally, it follows, *they* are no good in case of a fire. Right?"

I shook my head.

"Okay. And the front steps. Well, just look for yourself and there is no need to say more. Sooooo—Rabbi Slutsky reasoned, and quite soundly it seems to me, why bother with a fire drill if there are no ways of getting out?"

Canelli noted the look of alarm in my face.

"Of course the Fire Department was not any more impressed with Rabbi Slutsky's reasoning than you seem to be."

"What did they do?"

"Closed the school down until Rabbi Slutsky promised to clear the back stairs of the books and have a fire drill."

"Ah, so that is why there are so many books in his room."

"Precisely. And that is why there is so much commotion over this list."

"But still, what are these different days for?"

"Oh, different teachers are having the fire drill on different days. Rabbi Slutsky feels he has gone along with a lot in consenting to clear the back stairs; to have the entire school have the drill on the same day is going too far. 'Think of the accidents that could happen,' he says. And since it is only make believe anyway there is no need for everyone to go at once."

I took a deep breath. "Canelli, this story makes me very nervous."

"Faith, Ellen, faith, like the Hasidic. They are basically optimistic and rely a lot on faith. They're a whole lot more mystical than other Orthodox Jews. Why, the Hasidic even believe in miracles."

"Okay, Canelli. I mean, I like Buber and dialogues and *I and Thou,* but what will I do in the event of fire? Tell me about the back staircase. Is it clear?"

"Yes, until we have Fire Drill Week. Then the books go back to the stairs so Rabbi Slutsky can reach his desk without climbing over mountains."

"What floor is my room, Canelli?"

"Second, back to back with me."

"Thank God for that."

"What a sweet thing to say."

"It's nice we'll be neighbors, Canelli, but I was just thinking that I probably can land alive with a second-floor jump."

"Ah, Ellen, you really don't have faith."

"Not even enough to escape fear, Canelli, let alone fire."

"But you must fight on our side against the Fire Department. Whenever word spreads that they're about to visit the school, we all run and remove the books from the back stairway so they won't shut us down."

"I'll fight the Fire Department if you promise to hold my hand when we jump from the burning building."

"Quiet out there, please," came a voice from the nearest office. "The rabbi is trying to conduct an interview for a prospective teacher of English studies."

We all hushed so we could overhear the telephone conversation.

"So tell me, Mr. Fleigelbaum, did you get a little college done? Good, good. And maybe you even graduated? Well, it's not necessary. You shouldn't feel bad. What's that you say? You've had experience with children?" Rabbi Slutsky shouted into the receiver. As he stood up, his dark blue-black suit shone in full display. "All right, Mr. Fleigelbaum, just two things more and we'll be done." Rabbi Slutsky assumed a firm tone and almost tripped on the pile of books barricading him. "Mr. Fleigelbaum, can you work Sunday mornings? Ah, excellent. And the last question. Are you married? Oh, Mr. Fleigelbaum, you disappoint me." Rabbi Slutsky pulled gently on his beard and scanned the ceiling for a few seconds, as he uprighted himself. "All right, Mr. Fleigelbaum, I'll make a deal. You sound like a good teacher. I'll give you a few weeks to find yourself a wife. How about it?"

At this point the other teachers were filing out of their rooms. Canelli pointed to his watch. "Come, it's three-thirty, time for English studies. I'll show you your room."

"What was that business about being married?"

"Don't worry. The rule refers only to male teachers, not females. I think I told you that for the men, marriage is a must."

"But was the Rabbi serious about the man's finding a wife within a few weeks?"

"Oh, perfectly. It's quite possible if he's Hasidic. They still have arranged marriages. So it's not crazy for Rabbi Slutsky to suggest that the man get married within a short time. Most of the girls you will be teaching have not yet met their husbands, but they usually marry right after graduation. You do know, of course, that they're not permitted to go on to college. Even the men, for that matter, can't go on with a secular education. They just continue religious studies. As for the women, it's straight to the kitchen."

"But wait, what about that dark woman in Rabbi Slutsky's room who asked us to be quiet?"

"Ruth?"

"I don't know her name but I saw a Phi Beta Kappa key dangling from a bracelet. Surely, she didn't get that for her cooking skills."

"Ah, Ruth is an unusual woman. First of all, she is not Hasidic, just Orthodox. And there is a very big difference. The Orthodox women are not forbidden to go to college, although Ruth did not actually enroll until a few years ago when the youngest of her five was Bar Mitzvahed."

"How old is her oldest?"

"Eighteen."

"What about Ruth?"

"She's thirty-five. Was married at sixteen, raised her family, and then started college. An amazing woman, truly. Do you know she majored in Greek? It's sad about the Phi Beta Kappa key."

"What do you mean?"

"Her husband makes her wear it with the diamond he had put on it. He is a diamond cutter, and he feels it's for both of them."

"What does she do here?"

"That is sad too—but just for Ruth, not for us. Here she heads the English studies, and if it weren't for her the girls would not learn a thing outside their Hebrew studies. But Ruth really loves literature, especially the Classics. She does not think literature is evil, as the Hasidic do. She's not so scared."

"Except of her husband!"

"Well, of course. That's why she is here. She could have had a job teaching at a university but he wouldn't hear of it. Too risky, he thought."

"And she went along with that?"

"Yes. Ruth is emancipated, but all is relative. She is still an Orthodox female, just not Hasidic."

"She's the only woman I've seen who looked attractive in the severe headpiece covering her hair."

"Ruth's a real Jewess. I always think of her as having stepped right out of the Bible."

She was beautiful, in a sad and haunting way. I guess it was her olive coloring, and her thick eyebrows, over those deep-set dark eyes. Even her long and narrow nose was beautiful.

"I tell her she's a Jewish madonna."

"Oh, Canelli."

"Sure, Ruth loves it. She tells me I'm a *goyishe kibbitzer.* Don't be put off by Ruth's dark wool dresses with their high collars and long sleeves. That's just standard Orthodox dress. She's very lively underneath that intense simplicity. Ruth is more like us than like the Hasidic. You'll see what I mean once you're here for a while. I don't even know how religious you are, Ellen, but I can tell you are not like the girls we teach. But despite all differences, I'm mad about them," Canelli confided in a lower voice. "Here are our rooms. As you can see, we're going to be roommates with only this thin partition separating your class from mine. I'd better warn you of something ahead of time. For some reason which I can't figure out, the girls enjoy coming into my class. They usually hide the chalk from your room if they get here before you so they can then run to me for some. So it's a good idea to always carry an extra piece with you. Here, have one. I took it from the public school where I teach. It's not so easy to come by supplies in this place."

"Thanks, Canelli. I can see you are a kindly neighbor. And remember, in case of fire, we go down together."

"If you remember that in case of the Fire Department, we clear the stairs together."

"Fair enough. Now I'd better go in."

"If you need any help, just lean hard on the blackboard and I'll come around."

I found the chaos pleasurable as once again I thought back to my own school days. I could still remember the hour when supplies were distributed and how Miss Beggs would reluctantly open her closet with her special supply closet key and parcel out the pads as if she had purchased the contents of her supply closet herself and was now being forced to deplete her savings. I could almost smell the new box of chalk as she removed the first piece from its nest of sawdust, all tight with the others like cigarettes in an unopened package. She never took more than one piece at a time, and as she extracted it I sensed her pleasure in its smoothness, which she examined before breaking the piece into two parts which by the end of the day would become dusty old stubs.

Now I saw there were about thirty girls in my class, aged sixteen and seventeen. I would estimate that about twenty-five of them were involved in some sort of fondling activity when I walked in. The other five were sleeping. I did not know exactly what to do as I watched them inserting pencils down each others' blouses, unzipping zippers, unbuttoning buttons, giggling, and laughing throughout with not a tinge of embarrassment.

What a contrast to the boys I had seen in the street. The boys, even at an early age, resemble old men; partly because of the way they dress and partly because they have no color. The girls looked healthy and rosy, and since single women are the only group among the Hasidic who do not wear any special type of clothing they are not distinguishable from any other group of female adolescents.

The girls continued to play, giggling and screaming whenever something or someone poked them in a ticklish spot. The gaiety with which the girls carried on these proceedings make me feel like a prig. Not only was I self-conscious to see sex going on in the classroom, but sex so open, so unconcealed, so unsymbolic and direct. It gave my literary mind a jolt to see something so unencumbered by artifice.

And yet for all of its refreshing qualities, the orgy was puzzling. What did the warnings about the Rabbi and his fanatically strict attitudes mean? I had been told that the girls were forbidden to read *Junior Scholastic* because it published girl-boy stories which were potentially stimulating. (Did the Rabbi object to things only potentially stimulating and not actually stimulating?) From a literary point of view I was completely in agreement about the ban on *Junior Scholastic,* but when I discovered that no distinction was made between that magazine and Shakespeare (who the Rabbi thought of as a source of anti-Semitism as well as sex), I had to protest.

A compromise was later worked out with Ruth's aid: I would be allowed to teach *Midsummer Night's Dream* but nothing from *Junior Scholastic*. For after all, the Rabbi said, how dangerous can a dream be—something that has nothing to do with daily life lived while awake. Fantasy, fairy tales, faith—they were all acceptable since they did not dictate how a man should conduct himself every day; they were not in the realm of religious law which for the Orthodox Jews is very concrete. In all likelihood, there is no place in the Talmud which specifically says the inserting of a pencil by one girl down another's blouse is wrong—which may be why it never occurred to Rabbi Levy to consider it so. Canelli put it best:

"Ellen, the first thing you've got to understand is that sex, for the Hasidic, is limited to what goes on between a man and a woman—at night, in bed—two weeks out of four."

"What about those other two weeks?"

"Nothing. Relations are forbidden during the week a woman menstruates and the week following, which she spends cleansing herself in the baths."

"And fondling other women?"

"Perhaps. But that's not sex. Sex needs a man and a woman to be sex since sex is only for creation. Actually, the taboo on relations coincides perfectly with the conceptual cycle. Here the Hasidic are like Catholics—no birth control permitted. That's why the families are so large. Six point something, I think."

"Come on, Canelli, that still doesn't explain the fondling in class."

"Sure it does. Look: given the definition that sex is for

having babies and that in order for that to happen both a
man and a woman are necessary, it follows with all the force
of Aristotelian logic that sex involving only one gender is
not really sex."

"Not Aristotelian logic, Canelli, Jewish logic."

"You see, for Rabbi Slutsky the physical contact of the girls
is a natural thing. It's like cuddling together for warmth
the way they did in the old country. The majority of Hasidic
Jews came here after World War II after being rounded up
from the concentrations camps by the survivors, who chose
this particular area because it already had a large ghetto of
Orthodox Jews."

"How many Hasidic live here?"

"Oh, about ten thousand. And remember, many of the girls
share their beds with each other. The sexes are separated,
starting at age 3." So the girls continued to fondle each other,
as if convinced, as I was eventually to become, that this was
play after a hard day's work at Hebrew studies—some little
break like high tea before starting the work at the end of the
day, the English studies where Rabbi Levy feared the real
source of corruption lay.

I went up to the blackboard and printed my name, for no
one can be a mere observer for too long without feeling left
out of things, and I was anxious to establish some contact
of my own, albeit less direct. The board shook with the pressure and shortly someone appeared from Mr. Canelli's side
of the partition to request that I please lean not so hard on the
chalk. Slowly the girls became calm, even curious.

"Are you our new teacher?" one inquired.

Recognition at last. I nodded, walked over to the desk, and perched upon the top.

"Are you married?"

"Do you wear a *sheitel?*"

"A what?"

"She means a wig. Are you Jewish?"

Questions came forth from everywhere. Again I thought back to my own school days and the forbidden quality of a teacher's private life.

"I will let you know all the answers when you get to know me, but I am still a stranger to you and you are still strangers to me. So first let's become friends and then slowly you will learn all you want to know."

Such a sensible little speech, I thought. But it would not do. It was obviously modeled too closely along the lines of Miss Beggs and Miss Topper and all the other old maids who had been my teachers. These girls were too free to play the role of pupil, especially with a woman, who is never an authority figure in their world. Consequently, I could not carry on like a little puppet pulling the strings of my own puppet pupils.

Questions continued; the girls seemed obsessed with my marital status. I suppose that since most of them were shortly to enter the state of matrimony themselves with men they had never met, their curiosity was not extraordinary at all but quite practical. In any event, I learned a good lesson from them—I plunged right into honesty.

"All right. If you will ask me one question at a time and introduce yourself when you do, I will tell you what you want to know."

"My name is Chava, and are you wearing a *sheitel,* I mean a wig?"

Chava pointed to her own red locks as if to clue me into the fact we were talking about hair.

"No, I am not wearing a *sheitel*. Is that the way you say it?"

"Yes, my name is Chana, and are you married?"

Again, I said no.

"That's why she's not wearing a *sheitel*," some self-appointed narrator explained.

"No," I corrected. "Even if I were married I wouldn't be wearing a wig."

"Then, you're not Jewish, Miss Frankfort, right?"

"That girl's Dvorah."

"And who's the narrator?"

"The what?" the narrator asked.

"You. The girl who fills me in with all the extra information. What is your name?"

"I am Sarah."

What a relief—a name I could easily pronounce. "I am Jewish, Sarah, but I am not religious."

"A *yiddishe goy,*" someone whispered.

"What's that?" I asked, but Sarah had already hushed the class since the phrase obviously carried some derision.

"She didn't mean it," Sarah said.

"Maybe she did," I answered. "And maybe she's right."

This time it was the girls who were surprised. Although women have little authority, adults, in general, are never to be contradicted or exposed. Certainly, not by themselves. And here I was exposing myself, which was probably more corrupting to the Hasidic values than hard core pornography.

By telling the girls what they wanted to know I had allowed myself to become initiated and in the process learned my next most important lesson—to be honest wherever possible and never to fall back on my role as a teacher in order to reenact some sacred pedagogue's fantasy of a necessary professional distance. Now that I had won their attention by demonstrating that I was willing to be human, it was time to get on with the business at hand—which was inquiring about what books they were using.

They used the standard high school *Adventure* series and this year it was *American Literature*. I asked them to take out their books and I was besieged with offers of a copy for myself. Most of the girls were already doubled up in their seats sharing books, and so I freely took the first one I was offered. In the index I spotted a nice neat phrase, "The Flowering of the New England Tradition." A bit teacherly, like my little speech, perhaps, but an easy start. I said it out loud.

"New England. What has that got to do with America? I'm Chana, could you please explain, Miss Frankfort?"

At first I did not follow the confusion and was myself confused. Then I discovered that most of the girls thought that New England was in England. So before taking on Emerson and his cronies, I took some time out for geography.

I was learning more than I was teaching. I saw that these girls did not think in my categories, like countries. They had, it is true, heard of England and America, as they called the United States, but their unit was not the country. It was the village. When I asked them where they came from, I was told the names of little villages in Marmaros, the eastern part of

Hungary, and the Unterland, the lower part of Hungary, towns I could locate only after I had consulted a map.

I wished I had a map in class to point out where we were located. In the minds of the girls Roebling Street or wherever they now resided was the equivalent of that small town in Marmaros with its shops, supported by its own rabbi who had come from that same town; all was still ordered around it as it had been known through the generations. I wanted to show them precisely where Brooklyn was, at least in relation to Manhattan, for although many of the girls had crossed the ocean to come to Roebling Street, few had crossed the river to Manhattan.

It was almost 5:30, time for dismissal. What, I wondered, would be the most enjoyable reading assignment. I selected an essay by Emerson: "On Friendship."

"Oh, no, Miss Frankfort. We can't read that."

"Why not?"

"Because we cannot take any books into our homes that are written in English."

"Then what do you read?"

"Hebrew for holidays or Yiddish."

"Anyway, I'm Sarah, remember? And I just wanted to tell you that we don't read too much because we are too busy helping take care of our sisters and brothers and fathers when we get home."

"What language do you speak at home?"

"My mother speaks Hungarian, my father Yiddish."

"Well Chana . . ."

"No, *Chava*."

"Well, Chava, how do you communicate in your house if your parents speak different languages?"

"It's Chava," she said, pronouncing the "Ch" in its proper way. "They both understand Yiddish and Hungarian. But anyway, my father does not talk to my mother that much."

I did not then understand that this was typical and in no way a sign of "lack of communication." That is, talk—serious talk—was reserved by men for members of their own sex. By using a different language they made sure that the women did not partake in men talk. The women spoke Hungarian, which the men used only when they wished to gossip or discuss daily matters with their wives, which usually meant meals.

"Very interesting, very interesting. But what can I assign you for homework if you can't take home your books?"

"Give us a composition."

"Okay, a composition you shall have. How about writing a description of someone you know well for whom you have strong feelings, either positive or negative?"

Blank looks. They did not understand the negative part.

"I mean a composition about someone you like." I cut out the negative option, since strong negative feelings about someone you know well are not considered possible among the Hasidic. Negative feelings are all reserved for that world outside, the one beyond Roebling Street.

When I left the school at 5:35 it was already dark. Little boys were walking home after their long day at school, loaded down with their Hebrew books. I passed the Zehlemer Butcher Shop and remembered that one of the girls had spoken of the Rebbe Zehlemer. Everything was so interwoven. Rebbe Zehlemer came from Zehlemer in Europe and he had his own congregation also from Zehlemer, which in turn had its own shops which helped to support the Rebbe whose Zehlemer School I then passed.

The butcher, a bearded man, was cleaning off the wooden carving block and removing the meat which hung from the hooks in the window. A few doors away was a tailor who was pulling down the strings to the lights above his machine. The most surprising bearded figure came next—the attendant at the corner gas station. It was the first time I had ever seen a bearded Jew in a menial occupation. He stood out as a real curiosity to me. It's one thing for a bearded Jew not to be a Talmudic scholar, but he should at least be a shopkeeper.

But the Hasidic did not feel that way. They had to have a self-sufficient community and since they forbade their young men to acquire secular educations, all those who did not come from a tradition of learning and scholarship which would qualify them for religious jobs had either to become little merchants or do menial labor, something which irritated the Orthodox non-Hasidic Jews. For them, a bearded Jew was the equivalent of a rabbi, at least in the eyes of the outside Gentile world, and they therefore thought it was degrading to the image of the Jew to have him working with his hands while he was wearing *payis,* the curly ear-locks.

I waited for the bus that would breeze me back into the city. The Williamsburg Bridge loomed over the neighborhood busy with the movement of the end of a day. The city was just beginning to sparkle with night while the little ghetto nestled beneath the bridge, oblivious to both the century and the city.

The next day Rabbi Levy advised me that the girls, they should get a little grammar, maybe. Inspired by his phrasing, I began a grammar lesson with the sentence, "The French, who are good cooks, can turn a simple meal into a gourmet's delight." My plan was to convey that the English language had provisions for pronouns, and that it is not always necessary to repeat the subject, as in my example "The French who" rather than "The French they." But no sooner had I started when an argument erupted.

"Oh no, Miss Frankfort, the Hungarians, they are the best cooks."

"She's lying because the Rumanians really are."

The French had fallen out of the running altogether and the grammar . . . well, the girls, they would maybe never learn any.

"Let's forget French and grammar and go on to the compositions you wrote for homework. Who would like to read hers?"

"Me."

"Okay. You're . . . ?"

"Dvorah, and this is about my father.

"My father, Moshe, sits and studies all day because he is a *batlan* and that is what *batlans* do because they can't do anything else because he was made out by G— to sit and study for Rebbe Himmelfarb in the synagogue. He is married to my mother Leah. My mother has six children and takes care of them and me and my father and I help her. The Rebbe pays my father Moshe most of the time because you know it costs money to live and how long can you just sit and think all day anyway? That is what my mother Leah wants to know when my father comes home. My father Moshe is a very good man and very smart, and that is why he is a *batlan* for Rebbe Himmelfarb and why I am proud of him because I don't know what else he would do, since all he knows is to sit and think. Sometimes my mother Leah says my father he should not think so much, but he still thinks. I think he's all right, and he is my father and I love him very much. This is the end of my composition now. I hope you got to know a little about my father Moshe, because he is a very good man and G— should only bless him so that he lives a long and happy life."

The other compositions were written in similar style, which I came to call conversational. Through them I learned of the various occupations associated with the Hasidic way of life. There was quite a hierarchy, ranging from the Rebbe, the local king complete with costume—a sable hat and silk slippers worn over white stockings covering the breeches, for what reason I do not know, except that it makes it harder to get the pants off and anything which makes the body less accessible is considered more spiritual—to the lowlier religious functionaries who preside over the ritual slaughtering of meats and chickens, circumcisions, ritual baths, and almost every other aspect of life. Even those activites which do not seem religious assume a religious aspect for the Hasidic, making possible more rules of behavior and jobs for people to see that the rules are correctly followed. This is one of the ways the Hasidic community seems to have gained its tremendous cohesiveness.

From the tone of the compositions I gathered that there was both love and fear of the fathers and sympathy for the mothers. But nowhere did I detect a single sentiment of rebellion or doubt. Yet the girls had no interest in converting me, just in explaining themselves. The Jews are not a proselytizing people; you must be born one or from one to be one and conversion will not do. Period.

Among the numerous descriptions of occupations—the *shohet*s (ritual slaughterers), the *shamashes* (religious servants of the house of worship), the *melamen* (instructors in religious matters), the *hazzan* (cantor), the *mohels* (circumcisers), and on and on and on—only one stood out like the piece of fruit among the vegetables in an I.Q. test.

"Who has a composition written in a different style? Okay, Chava, let's hear yours. What's it about?"

"The Most Unforgettable Character I Have Known."

"And who is that, Chava?"

"It's a country doctor in Kansas who makes house calls during torpedoes."

"Torpedoes? Do you mean tornadoes?"

"Can I tell you tomorrow, Miss Frankfort?"

"Just tell me today how you got to know such a character, since you are forbidden to bring the *Reader's Digest* home?"

"Oh, we can take home magazines, Miss Frankfort, just not books."

"Sit down, Chava. I want to say a few things before we go on." I took a deep breath and assumed my most serious mien.

"This is the first time I have ever taught in a religious school. Naturally, I expect the students to be pious, honest people. And instead what do I find? Lying, cheating, plagiarism. On a grand scale! Where are your ethics?" I called out, a bit carried away by my own fervor.

They looked blank.

"Do you want the Jewish religion to have a bad name?"

"It already has one."

"Okay. If you are not concerned with principles, then at least pay attention to strategy. There are good ways of cheating and bad ones. You know, cheating is like all other disciplines. You don't just sit down and cheat any sloppy old way you please. First you carefully consider the matter of text. If you are going to copy someone else's work, you shouldn't pick anything too conspicuous. Like Kansas and country doctors. Then there is the matter of vocabulary. Before you use such words, you should learn the difference between a *tornado* and a *torpedo*."

Now the girls were starting to respond. By the time I finished my speech, several came up to thank me for handing out shrewd hints. And free, no less! I immediately made a note to teach about sarcasm and satire the very next day.

But on my way home I came across something which made me change my mind. I had stopped at a corner newspaper stand. I was curious to see what the sources of communication were after learning that day that not only were books written in English forbidden in the home, but television sets and radios too. Was there anything at the newsstand that was not taboo? I was given a copy of *Der Yid*, a biweekly paper, but I could not read it because it was in Yiddish. Evidently other Jewish papers that I had heard of like *The Forward* were considered off limits too because they were not sympathetic to the Hasidic, who felt the Yiddish press spread lies about them.

I did, however, discover one source of communication I could understand. It was a circular, written in English, which was posted in a neighborhood store and which I purchased from the owner. It had a general air of intimacy based on the assumption that its readers all shared the same values, as well as a total disregard for objectivity, not unlike some of the underground papers a few years later.

I sat down with the circular, anxious to learn about the world as my girls saw it for it was obvious that my own world —the American one of pumpkin pies and Miss Beggs and Miss Topper—was as alien to the girls as Mars. At first I was put off by the odd form of advertising. "If someone should, God forbid, have to die, please rest assured that the God-fearing house of Moshe Zevi Klein and his sons could take care of everything so it is absolutely kosher. We of course wish no one to die, God forbid, but just in case, we are ready. We wish you all health. The House of Moshe Zevi Klein and Sons."

The ads were spread throughout little vignettes called "faith strengtheners." The first I read concerned a concentration camp prisoner who is recalling for his readers the time a vision came to him late at night, directing him to his friend who was already in the ovens. He feared for his own life, but when he recognized the vision as that of the dead man's grandfather he snuck out and made his way to the place where the ovens were. There he found his friend, David, dead as could be. He called his name many times, telling him that he had just been in touch with his grandfather, who told him that a miracle was shortly to revive him. Finally the dead man started to gasp for breath, asking many times to have the message repeated. When he revived he explained that the reason he asked to have the message repeated was not because he did not hear it the first time, but that each hearing gave him more strength. Both the former dead man and his savior were well and living in the Hasidic community.

But not everything turned out so happily. For in the same

circular there was a brief sketch of a Rebbe who had just died. His whole life was described on the page—his years in the concentration camp before his heroic escape, his coming to this country with his large family, his rise to head one of the biggest Hasidic summer colonies, and finally his death at the age of fifty-seven of a coronary. "So goes the six millionth and first victim of Hitler" was the last sentence. And so went my desire to teach about sarcasm and cynicism. Who could make distinctions between truth and delusion, reality and madness after concentration camps?

Instead of teaching about irony the next day, I stuck close to the text, hoping to awaken the imagination of the girls to the world of feelings that others had experienced and written about. The irony which only I could appreciate was that although I could not get to them, they got to me. I felt their sense of joy, their pride in having survived, and their determination which had made survival possible. And above all, their faith.

The day we marked the regents examinations was full of revelations.

Said Canelli, "You don't think we take the Regents seriously. The only reason we go through the motions is so the school can be accredited."

"You mean the marks have no significance?"

"To nobody but the girls who take them very seriously, which is why we bother with exact grades like 77 or 83."

"Why do they care if they're not going on to schools or applying for anything?"

"Probably all those years of watching their mothers haggle

over a penny or two with the grocer has conditioned them to fight over a point or two."

One girl chose the topic, "Labor Problems Today" and proceeded to tell about the troubles her mother had in giving birth to her brother, the third from the last.

Another picked, "Should Billboards Be Abolished?" and went on to argue that they should because if boys didn't have billboard alleys to go to, they would not get into trouble so much.

All the teachers wondered, "Should Radio, Television, and Books Written in English Be Abolished?" and could have written essays on that topic.

Canelli contributed his share of lines from the History Regents, which contained a question on Israel's role in a current issue. Most of the girls spent hours pouring out the entire history of the Jews, ignoring the topic entirely. At one point Rabbi Slutsky stormed into the room, his red beard flying like the tail of a runaway horse, warning the girls to ignore the question on Israel since it did not exist. (The Hasidic Jews do not recognize the state of Israel since it was formed before the coming of the Messiah.) After Rabbi Slutsky left, the girls went back to the question, not out of any desire to be sacrilegious but merely out of pride. They agreed not to mention Israel and crossed out the word wherever it had been used. But they refused to pass up an opportunity to pour forth something they knew well, the history of the Jews.

It turned out that I was not the only teacher with a missionary soul, trying endlessly and in vain to bring Western culture to Williamsburg. There was another teacher of English, and

Adam Lowry was his name. Adam wanted to spread the message about love and life and freedom and beauty. Nothing less, nothing more. Adam wore a nonrabbinical beatnik beard, but a lack of acquaintance with Greenwich Village made it impossible for Rabbi Slutsky to recognize the difference. Similarly, it was sheer ignorance which made him see the one earring Adam wore as Hungarian. How Rabbi Slutsky worked Adam's motorcycle into the refugee image I'll never know. Adam was pleasant enough although his slightly schizy smile was disconcerting. But Rabbi Slutsky considered him safe because he was married.

Adam wanted to teach the girls about poetry, the language of the soul, and one day he brought in his own poetic creations, which explored the principle of free love. The girls were confused. All their lives they had heard that in this world you get nothing for nothing. So what could Adam mean? The more literal among them decided that he meant your father makes a deal with your fiancé to marry you without a dowry. But when Adam started to talk about the joys of the body in experiencing the soul, some of the girls began to sense that they had misunderstood him.

Most of the girls had wonderfully trained noses for sniffing out the forbidden (all those distinctions between kosher and *trafe* were not for nought), and whenever they found a scent they ran to Rabbi Kabulowsky, an important teacher of Hebrew studies, as he directed them to do. He had an even bigger and better nose for getting right to the source of the smell. First he would sit the girls around him as he sprawled in his long black rabbinical garb. He would place his chubby hands on his knees, spread his legs, and lean forward, insisting that the girls omit not a single detail. When they had presented all the facts, Rabbi Kabulowsky would give a lesson on why what was taught was not kosher, if you know what I mean.

Adam was ultimately fired, not because he taught free love but because he practiced it, as Rabbi Slutsky discovered when he called his house and the startled girl who answered said she was not Adam's wife, Adam had no wife, and who was this calling anyway?

The school almost lost another teacher, a former Rhodes scholar who spent hours trying to teach the girls grammar. In vain she would demonstrate why the verb "to be" takes the predicative nominative and not the objective. But they were not interested. At moments of extreme hopelessness she would threaten to leave. "I shall return to Oxford if you keep this up." And the girls would answer, "Who is Oxford?" imagining the most romantic of all possibilities. But she stayed on because compared to the British she found the girls warm, and anyway, she disapproved of acts of desertion.

I had been working at the Yeshiva for a few months and had not yet received my salary. I had been told that as the newest teacher I would have to wait until the records were in order, which seemed as long and drawn out a process as waiting for the Messiah.

Finally one Thursday I found an envelope with a check in it, signed with a big scrawl by Rabbi Slutsky himself: "See, I told you not to worry."

Rabbi Slutsky tried to be fair. Each month he paid a different group of teachers. Those lucky enough to receive checks that day were hurrying out to cash them. What was the rush? The banks were open late on Thursdays and I was confident there would be time to cash my check after classes at the end of the day.

As soon as I identified my employer, a nearby store refused to touch the check. Reluctantly I crossed the street to a place that charged a fee for cashing checks, certain that they would be pleased to accommodate me. But I was wrong. They advised me to try the bank where the Yeshiva had its account and gave me directions on how to find it.

By now the neighborhood was familiar, and the distinctive dress of the residents did not seem so unusual. I passed the bearded men, their maleness heavily guarded by layers of clothing, and the little boys who, though fair in coloring, always looked sickly. Then I spotted a familiar face.

"Canelli, what a godsend. I'm sure you can help direct me to the bank which houses the school finances."

"Why are you going there?"

"To cash my check. None around here is willing."

"We don't have the best credit record in town, I'm afraid."

"Hey, Canelli, who's that man ahead of us?"

"He's Rebbe Zehlinsky, the Hasidic Pope. You wouldn't understand, Ellen. You have to be Catholic to appreciate it. Look at all his clothing. Hasidim are just like us. The higher you go in the hierarchy, the less accessible the body becomes."

"I didn't even realize there was a hierarchy."

"How many men have you seen with sable hats on their heads and silk slippers worn over white stockings? If you become really keen, you can guess a male's occupation by his dress. See the pockets sewn on the back of the Rebbe's silk coat? That's not an arbitrary whim of fashion. There aren't many like that. Most of the men have plain long overcoats, and if they're fairly high up they may have a large-brimmed hat made of beaver."

"Like that one over there?"

"Yes."

"But suppose you're not a Pope or something high up? With what do you cover your head?"

"With your own humble hair."

"Thank God the Hasidic have so much, or those less blessed would freeze their ears off."

"What's interesting is that the male clothing, for all its symbolic importance, is not the basis of status in this community. Just its reflection."

"What is the basis of status?"

"It's very nice. Status is based on how religious you are and you are granted the honor of dressing in a regal manner only if you've proven that you live the life of a perfect Hasid. There is a very wealthy member in this community who has high status, which is unusual since his occupation has nothing to do with religion and therefore he should rank low. But because he *uses* his money to make himself more religious, he can dress like a Hebrew teacher. See what I mean?"

"Tell me, how does one use money to become more religious?"

"First you buy two sinks. Then when you make more money, you buy two iceboxes. And now this guy even has two stoves, which means he has the ultimate insurance that meat will *never* mix with dairy. And as a last gesture he contributes generously to the congregation of Rebbe Zehlinsky. Now, listen, Ellen. Be careful. We're leaving the Jewish section of the ghetto. The bank is about three blocks ahead but it's very tiny so look out for it."

Canelli and Rebbe Zehlinsky both disappeared from sight once I left the confines of the Jewish section. I made my way along the wharf under the Williamsburg Bridge, where the city in its more melodramatic aspects appeared, its dark warehouses and factories giving forth chemical odors, the dust, the dirt, the noise, and above all, movement—movement of trucks, movement of workers, and seizures of kids clustered about corner candy stores, waiting for something which might not arrive. What a contrast to the Jewish children, who scurried home like little animals returning to nests. Never once did I see a group of Hasidic boys just standing about anywhere.

The bank was in an out-of-the-way spot, almost as if it was not supposed to be found, and indeed I nearly didn't find it. What a poor little miserable bank it was. The clerk inside referred me to the banker, a red-faced chap whose cheap double-breasted dark gabardine suit shone like Rabbi Slutsky's and, like the Rabbi's, was buttoned from right to left. I entered the decrepit cubicle he occupied and explained that I would like to cash my pay check.

"When did you receive it?" he asked.

"Just this afternoon."

"Just this afternoon, you say? The very same hour is often too late. Go back and next month be the first one here. Then we'll be in a better position to service you."

I sat there in disbelief. One would have thought the check

was for some mighty sum, not the mere sixty dollars I was being paid for one month's work.

Had I the faith of the Hasidic I might have been able to manage on so little. But I could not. Reluctantly, I decided that I would have to leave at the end of the term. And what's more, I reasoned with full Talmudic style, I now had some experience on my record which would be helpful in seeking new work.

When I told Rabbi Slutsky of my plans to leave, he promised to pay me the very first thing next month all that he owed me. But my mind was set and he could not change it. I was sincere when I told him how much I would miss the school.

"I have only one request."

"*Nu?*" he asked, shrugging his shoulders in his usual manner to make clear that he could promise me nothing.

"Please do not tell the girls yet."

"So, you don't want I should tell them, I won't."

It was a simple request and Rabbi Slutsky nodded that he would go along with it.

As I left Rabbi Slutsky's office, Canelli saw me.

"What are you doing having conferences with Slutsky?"

"Serious business, my friend. I'm leaving."

"Are you serious about this serious business?"

"Deadly. But you mustn't tell a soul. Even Rabbi Slutsky agreed to grant that request."

"Why shouldn't he? It doesn't cost him anything. What I want to know is why you are leaving?"

"It's simple, Canelli. I can't afford to work here any longer. Don't forget you have this job just to supplement your other.

A little pocket money for pins. Anyway, I'm not leaving yet and when I do we'll keep in touch. And now, I must go teach a lesson on the 'Flowering of New England Tradition.' "

I don't know how it happened, but the girls did discover that I was leaving. From that point on there was little teaching to be done. It is true that I had expected the news to be disruptive, but I did not understand why all teaching had to come to a complete halt. It never occurred to me that the reason was that the girls assumed I was getting married. Why else would I be leaving them?

Perhaps it was a lesson on Emerson that led them astray. We had been reading his essay on gifts. The girls did not approve of his notion that the only suitable gift—that is, the only one expressive of real feelings—is a handmade object or freshly picked flowers. First of all, the whole thing was not practical; there were no fresh flowers in Williamsburg. And what's more, how about diamonds? They are not hand picked (although many of the girls had relatives who worked at diamond cutting and in this direct way could almost make diamonds meet Emerson's requirements). Finally, out of exasperation, one girl asked, "Look, Miss Frankfort, if you were engaged, what would you want? A flower or a diamond?"

A few days later as I walked into the class I immediately sensed something unusual was going on. It did not take any great sensitivity for hardly was I seated when some girls came running up and lifted me, chair and all, into the air. The rest of the class started singing and dancing around the room while I remained up in the air trying to hold onto the arms of the chair, having already let go of my dignity.

"Let me down, let me down, please let me down," I pleaded. But the girls did not heed my pleas and continued to carry me around while I tried to figure out what had taken possession of their senses. A special Jewish holiday I was not aware of? Did the Messiah arrive while I was on my way to school? Anything seemed feasible. "What's going on? Won't someone, anyone tell me?"

In response to my cries, Sarah ran up to the blackboard and scribbled out a translation of the songs being sung.

My soul and skill into the melody I poured;
It leaped and danced and rose and soared
Into a world of gladness sans alloy,
And all it sang was joy, joy, joy!

And is it in my tongue to tell
The mighty pulse and swell
Of exaltation lifting every heart and glance,
Shining from every countenance,
That wedding night?

The Holy One beckons to ascend
To where both love and fear do blend
And flow a single tide
In rapture unified.

I played my song, my happy song;
And all the wedding throng
A while sat still, entranced,
Then rose together, clapped their hands and danced.
Ah! To lift the heart forlorn to hope and bliss:
What greater joy than this!

"So now I get it. Someone is getting married. How wonderful! But if you want me to share your festivities—if you want me to survive them—won't you please let me down so I can congratulate the lucky girl?"

They almost dropped me and my chair. But then they realized I must be teasing them.

"Don't be shy, Miss Frankfort. We know anyway," Sarah said.

"Okay, but let me down." At this point I was willing to agree to anything as long as they put my chair back on the ground.

"*Mazel tov, mazel tov,*" they all began to chant once I was down.

Leaning back in my chair, with the hard wood behind and the firm floor below, the festivity hit home with the force of reality. It was *I*, not they, who was getting married. And it was for *me* that all this was being done!

My first response was to flee the scene. A quick consultation with Rabbi Kabulowsky. Anything. But all I had to work with was my own wits.

The celebration proceeded unhampered by my refusal to acknowledge the forthcoming event, which the girls concluded was due to a peculiar shyness not unlike the New England tradition with its lack of ostentation, its simplicity, and its high premium on the sane and rational. No, they had never had much sympathy for Emerson. And Thoreau they considered a real *meshugeneh.* Who would ever go off by himself to learn about ants and leave his loved ones behind? The flowering of New England had been my undoing, no doubt.

I still had not decided on a course of action when the next part of the drama rolled forth. Now it is one thing to be lifted in the air and carried about; that position is a bit uncomfortable and conducive to dizziness, but it does not lead to lies and moral crises which must be resolved on the spot. What took place next made me want to escape the whole scene even more and never again face the world of the *shtetl*. The girls started to pile gifts before me, one larger than the other, eyeing me throughout. And then, knowing that I would now have to acknowledge the event, the class became quiet.

While they waited to see which gift I would untie first, I wanted to say, "Look, I think there's been some mistake." But how was I to tell them that? The truth, the real world, my world, the world outside theirs, would never be known to them, and to thrust it upon them now seemed pointless. My only hope was to go along with the charade in a way that would be convincing.

On the top of the largest package was a card. I read it aloud: "Aren't you glad we didn't take Emerson too seriously? Lots of love and happiness and richness for a happy and long life for you and your husband you're going to marry and God should only bless you both forever."

I blushed for reasons very different from the ones the girls assumed were embarrassing me and then proceeded to open the largest present. How unfortunate that they had dismissed Emerson so fast, I thought, as I made my way through lots of newspaper. For a minute I had hopes of receiving something practical, a pot, perhaps, which, like all utensils the Hasidic use, would have been ritually bathed upon purchase; the local hardware store had on its premises facilities for such ceremonies. At least, there was something imaginative, if not handmade, about a pot receiving a ritual bath.

But no. As I made my way through the newspaper it became apparent that the girls thought I deserved something better. Out emerged a large fake crystal glass piece in two parts. The first was the cover, which had a fluted glass knob at its tip similar to the four knobs at the bottom of the second piece, a bowl. I placed the top on the bowl and fulfilled the fantasy of every girl sitting in anticipation of the climax of her life. The other gifts were more modest—a candle holder made out of Ikora, and another fake crystal piece, this one a cake plate. For a while I forgot the hoax that prompted the gifts and was touched that the girls had bought them with their spare pennies. I no longer felt a fake; I would not have chosen these gifts for myself even if I were getting married, but as mementos of the girls, I would appreciate them even if my single state lasted forever.

Now came a more difficult time—*my* turn to give. And what the girls wanted in exchange for the gifts (again a flagrant contempt for Emerson's notion of gifts never given in order to receive) was information about HIM.

As on the first day, questions started to fly forth from the girls as they moved up closer and huddled cosily together in pairs.

"Have you ever seen him, Miss Frankfort?"

"Who is the *shadchan* who arranged the match?"

"Is he defective?"

"Defective? What do you mean by defective? Why do you think I would marry someone defective?"

"No, we mean does he have any non-Jewish blood in him?"

"Through which *shadchan*, Miss Frankfort?"

"What is a *shadchan*?"

"Oh, you know, a matchmaker."

"Where is the wedding going to be held? A hall? A temple? The street? Are the men going to be allowed to mix with the women?"

"How can you have a marriage if the men and women don't mix?"

"You see, Miss Frankfort, in our synagogues the men and women can never be together. The men are in one room, the women in another."

"How can they dance, then?"

"What do you mean?" Chana asked.

"I always thought the Hasidic weddings have a lot of dancing."

"Yes, they do. But only the men."

What the girls were telling me about Hasidic weddings seemed less real than my own hypothetical one.

"Well, at my wedding men and women will be together."

They understood; for after all, I was a *yiddishe goy,* so what could you expect? But a wedding was a wedding no matter who you were, and there were certain questions still unanswered. I told them that I was getting married in the office of a clerk. The girls decided that this was just another peculiar custom of *yiddishe goyim,* and of course they were right.

"Miss Frankfort, what does your wedding gown look like?" they asked, the image of marriage in a municipal office not imprinted on their minds.

"A very simple dress, girls. Beige, silk shantung."

"Who will check it for the *shatnes* law?"

"What's that?"

"Oh, you know, Miss Frankfort. Someone has to go through the seams of clothing to see that there is no linen mixed in with the wool."

"How many people are there going to be?"

"Oh, not too many. A small ceremony," I answered, as I thought of marriages to which I had been invited as the fourth legal necessity in City Hall.

Up until now there had been little self-consciousness, but one must allow for some awkwardness in reaching a climax and the first sign they were ascending were their titters.

"You ask her, Chava."

"No, why don't you, Chana?"

"Miss Frankfort, Chana and Chava want to know where you'll be the first night."

"You haven't told us whether the room is in the apartment with your mother or whether it is above or below?"

"Neither," I said. The girls interpreted that as a few floors apart or maybe a block away, allowing for the fact I was a *yiddishe goy*.

Giggles.

"What is the date of the wedding?"

"That's a secret."

"Will you tell us if we promise not to visit you the following morning?"

"Why do you look surprised, Miss Frankfort? We always do that. Not just for you."

"Oh, leave Miss Frankfort alone, Chava. Look how she's blushing."

"I'm sorry, Miss Frankfort, and I didn't mean to embarrass you. Want us to help you carry the presents down?"

"Okay. Let's first throw away the newspaper wrapping."

"Can I have it, Miss Frankfort? My father saves paper."

"Sure, Dvorah, help yourself."

Saturday

Dear Canelli,

I am writing this letter the morning after the afternoon when I didn't have a chance to say farewell. There is so much I wanted to talk to you about that I am settling for the written word. And with luck and lack of laziness, let it be the start of a lengthy correspondence. Doubtless, you heard about yesterday's wedding celebration. Do not be deceived. The whole thing was a fake as far as facts are concerned. Of course, when it comes to fantasy, what relevance does fraud have?

As I made my way to the bus loaded down with my wedding presents, I felt confused. Life for the girls is so simple; they know exactly what is in store for them. It's all there for them to follow like a numbered painting and no one seems to question the design. Except me, dear Canelli.

What is my own? While riding on the bus I began to feel as I did when the college president spoke of her dedication to work. There was the same sensation that neither the girls nor she had ever experienced doubt about what they were going to do with their lives. Both had security. For the college president, an old New England type, work has always been the answer. For these girls, children of European peasants, work, too, is the answer. Only work is defined differently. No education is required for the work of the home and the work of rais-

ing a family whose life centers about religion. Both the Hasidic girls and the college president have something in common—a guiding principle which they never question and which roots them in a tradition.

As for myself, Canelli, what am I to do with my life? What are my guiding principles, my sources, my roots? And what on earth am I to do with these damn boxes of gifts? I really do not have room for them yet I can't throw them away. I guess they're like souvenirs of a time spent in a different world where I saw a way of life I never dreamed existed so close. For a moment I fell into a fit of humility from which I emerged depressed.

Of course, all my friends are in the same situation so I can't indulge in feelings of isolation. I'll probably return to the worlds from which I've come—those of publishing and advertising and the academe, where people are skeptical, cynical, bitter about selling out—worlds where everyone wants to lead a good life even though they no longer believe it's possible. And over cocktails, Canelli, I'll tell quaint tales of girls I once taught who never knew uncertainty, and even my less skeptical friends will think I am exaggerating.

But do the girls turn out any happier than we do? Or is it ignorance that makes them unaware of their frustrations? It certainly does not seem that way to me. But then I've seen them at the peak, before their lives are culminated and sealed into a routine forever. Perhaps they are no different from medieval peasants. How much of my view of the girls is a romantic one? They strike me as happy, but is it the happiness of a child who has never experienced puberty, and indeed, except for those hormones which never stop working during English classes, the girls are prepubertal in their emotions. But so are their mothers and grandmothers. Nobody, it seems, has ever rebelled, ever questioned, ever grown up.

In college I read of many people who thought that that was the ideal. But again I wonder, Canelli. Do these girls have good sex lives? Do they enjoy their roles as women? Are they free? These are questions I have not been able to answer, but I am still curious about them. Maybe you can give me your private insights.

Anyway, once at home I removed a ceramic dish from my teak bench and replaced it with the fake crystal bowl. The candlestick holders I set upon my thrift shop marble top table and I think it was around then that I saw my life as a mishmash. The thought, not new, nevertheless kept me from falling asleep. I lay tossing and turning without going anywhere. From time to time I came upon the realization that I am not as free from the concerns that dominate the lives of my girls as I had thought. With each realization, I repeated three times in a sweet ritualistic way, "I am an emancipated woman." If only the hideous bowl would turn into a ball, even though it's fake crystal, in exchange for its clairvoyance I would keep it on permanent display.

By morning the educated emancipated college graduate revived, removed the crystal bowl from the teak table, replaced it with the ceramic dish, and acknowledged that an unknown future is part of what makes life exciting. Unknown job prospects I could live without, but they go along with the setup. If teaching at the Yeshiva has thrown me off because the girls are so authentic, my life is no less real because it's something else. But what, Canelli? You know, I really did enjoy the work, and I've decided I'd like another job teaching. If possible I'd like it in a private school again. My only request is that it be located in this century. How's that for sanity?

Tuesday

Ellen!

First, my sweet former neighbor behind the blackboard, this is no farewell. I intend to remain friends even though a partition of several miles now separates us. Has air ever interfered with the movement of mail?

Second, your wedding ceremony was no charade but merely a rehearsal for that happy moment when. . . . Not that I think you can't survive without marriage. You are not a Hasidic woman or even an Orthodox Jewess. After so short a stay at the Yeshiva, I'm not sure you can appreciate what marriage means to the girls. In a way, marriage is a way of never growing up, of never having to be alone, of always having a family around you. Marriage is a way of insuring that life will go on as the girls have always known it, which is why the Hasidic women visit the bride the morning after her wedding. For them it is not snooping but is rather the only way they can recapture the memory of the most important day in their lives, a brief moment when they can borrow some of the bride's romance while it is still ripe and abundant, for how quickly the magic disappears and how soon life for the women becomes routine. But on that one morning the miracle of being newly wed still lingers, at least in the imagination, and that

.55.

*is why the morning is shared. You mustn't forget that the
women are forbidden to continue their education.*

*So it isn't any wonder that the girls were curious about your
imagined marriage. All their lives they've been taught to think
of little else. Did you know that Hasidic girls are not permitted a Bas Mitzvah because girls are simply not important
enough for any special ceremony except that which makes a
woman into a wife, and hence, worthwhile.*

*Birthday celebrations are also forbidden, but with some ex-
travagant display of equality they are forbidden to both boys
and girls on the grounds that birthdays have nothing to do
with religion. Are you beginning to see why marriage is so
special? Only by marrying can a mother and daughter become
equals. Only then can each understand what the other has
gone through. The marriage bond cements mother and daughter far more than it does husband and wife in a world where
ideas of morality rarely extend beyond taking care of a mother
when she is old and frail and can no longer bring up children,
hers or her daughters'. Hasidic mothers are entitled to become
children again and to receive the mothering they once so self-
lessly (according to them) gave. In this way, no one ever
grows old and years are passages back to childhood. The only
period omitted in the cycle is adolescence, a necessary gap for
the Hasidic way of life. For how else are you going to keep the
kids from wanting to cross that river away from the ghetto?
Only by snuffing out the period in life when rebellious feelings are alive and by making religious even those activities
which don't seem religious to you and me—the slaughtering
of meats, the slicing of boys, and the bathing of women.*

Maybe that's because there's very little other-worldly emphasis. The stress is strictly on making it from day to day, a monumental enough task in itself. Wondering about futures becomes a hindrance to the job at hand—daily life. Even the religious laws are closely interwoven with day-to-day rules of conduct. The Hasidic are not like the Amish or other surviving sects. They fully accept commercialism. To refuse to become assimilated is one thing, quite proper, but to ignore technology is sheer stupidity. If you insist on taking a horse and buggy to the synagogue rather than a car, you just spend a longer time traveling and a shorter time praying.

How about ending here with that Hasidic wisdom. But only for the time being. I shall be expecting regular progress reports on daily crises which you naturally overcome in Hasidic style, and if the opportunity arises, a little more information for my own Jewish studies. In the meantime I offer you all the warmth and wisdom of the sun.

·○·❧ANDREWS❧·○·

MY JOB PLACEMENT counselor was very encouraging. An interesting opening had just come through and there was a possibility that I might qualify. It was a job at a private girls' school in Manhattan teaching English to the Upper Forms.

"What are the Upper Forms?" I asked.

"That's the equivalent of high school."

"I see," I said, and put the term on a pile set aside for vocabulary that's private to private schools, varying slightly from each to each in order to distinguish themselves not only from the public schools but from one another.

"I have just had experience with that age range," I said, careful to use neutral vocabulary.

"Well, I'll be frank with you," the counselor said uncomfortably. "It's just your experience which concerns me. Not the fact, of course, that you have had some. That is all to your advantage. It's a question of where it was. If I were you I would go easy on the Yeshiva. Don't lie, of course. I'd never want to counsel any of my girls to do that. But there is no harm done by underplaying it, perhaps not even mentioning it unless you must. Private schools are very parochial in their own fashion, Miss Frankfort, and they just might not understand. Also, one last word of advice. You needn't follow it, of course, but it might be wise for you to wear a conservative suit, something along the navy blue lines, and a hat, if at all possible."

After our brief chat, the counselor called the Andrews School, spoke to the secretary of the headmistress, said that she had a very fine candidate for them to meet, and set up an appointment for the very next day.

I opened the heavy Tudor type door of the old brownstone that had housed generations of Andrews girls and Miss Agatha B. Langley, headmistress, who had managed to outlive generations. The large door resounded upon closing and a deep voice echoed out from somewhere, "Miss Frankfort, do come right in." Timidly I approached the room from which the voice had come—a large room with a fireplace, an old Persian rug, and a paneled ceiling under whose beams Miss Langley sat.

"How do you do?" Miss Langley stood up to shake my hand, towering over me and my hatless head before offering me a seat. "Tell me, Miss Frankfort, what has been your previous teaching experience?"

I thought of the placement counselor and her advice to go easy on the Yeshiva. Mention it only if it's absolutely necessary. It now seemed absolutely necessary. That is, some experience, even that at the old Yeshiva, seemed better than none.

"I was formerly employed as a teacher at . . . the . . . uh . . . a Hebrew sort of Seminary of America." The last part I blurted out very rapidly, stressing the "America."

"I see. Could you tell me about it, Miss Frankfort? I don't quite recall having heard of it."

"Well, it's a most interesting institution. Quite international in atmosphere, you might say."

"Do they require the girls to study Latin and Greek?"

"No, I would say the concentration is more on English."

"That sounds quite progressive indeed. We at the Andrews School are considering a similar change in our curriculum. What are your own views on the matter?"

"Oh, I favor speaking English—that is, I mean, I favor concentrating on English. That is, I mean, I am not totally convinced that Latin and Greek are necessary in the contemporary curriculum."

"I believe in being honest, Miss Frankfort, I am going to tell you why we have an opening in the middle of the year. The teacher who left had a nervous breakdown. I am not convinced that our girls did not help to bring about that sorry state of affairs. I am telling you this because I sense a strength of character in you that our dear little Miss Hillson did not possess. She knew poetry very well, grammar perfectly. In short, she was quite a scholar. I don't know if you are or not, although you come well recommended by your college. But I do sense you can handle a classroom situation without having your nerves shattered. Am I correct?"

I thought the fact that I could handle Miss Langley without having my nerves shattered was sufficient proof of my toughness.

"Yes, there is a directness in your manner that impresses me favorably. You just might very well be what we need here at Andrews. Of course, we do have several more people to meet, and I can make no final decision before seeing all the other candidates."

We shook hands. As I was about to leave, Miss Langley called me back to her desk. "One more matter, Miss Frankfort. As a formality, it will be necessary to speak to the head of the seminary where you have taught. I would appreciate your giving the telephone number to my secretary so we may contact them should our decision call for it."

I winced as I prepared to hand over the number to the secretary whom Miss Langley had summoned.

"Miss Millet, this is Miss Frankfort, a prospective teacher. I have asked her to give you the telephone number of the school with which she was formerly affiliated. I do not think it is in our directory of private schools. And Miss Millet, you might give Miss Frankfort one of our own bulletins so she can learn a little about us. After all, prospective employees have just as much a right to investigate their employers as the reverse," Miss Langley said, as if she were making an amendment to the Bill of Rights.

The next few days were filled with a special form of horror. I could not help but imagine the telephone conversation between the Yeshiva and the Andrews School. Over and over again I could hear it start:

First Miss Millet. Softly she would say, "I am calling for the Andrews School. May I speak to the headmistress please?"

"Vat? Who's a headmistress? There is no such thing here."

"I'll talk to whoever is the head, please."

"Maybe you should mean Rabbi Slutsky. He's like the head. Rabbi Slutsky, are you around somewhere for the phone? All right, *mamaleh,* here comes your head."

Miss Millet would wait to hear the phone change hands. "Am I speaking to the principal?"

"Right."

"This is Miss Millet of the Andrews School."

"Vat?"

"Hello? Pardon, yes, Miss Millet of the Andrews School."

"The Andrews School. I should know. So vat do you want with me, Miss Andrews School?"

Finally I decided that I would look for another job as soon as I had heard officially from the Andrews School. Probably Miss Langley herself would call to inform me that someone better qualified than I had been chosen for the job. And then she would wish me well.

The call came. It was Miss Langley. She told me I had the job.

Friday

Help, Canelli, help,

I am hiding out in the former servants' quarters of an elegant old brownstone waiting for the headmistress of the house which is now a school to escort me to the Friday afternoon faculty conference where I will be united with the rest of the Andrews faculty for better or perhaps even worse.

I may be more out of place here than at the dear old Yeshiva, but so far I have been able to "pass." Let me spill out some impressions onto your ever open Italian ears. I mean let me be a yenta *while no one is listening, for in a few minutes I'll have to become Waspy. But not too, because old Langley is 6-feet-full of the New England tradition (grossly overgrown) and does not like people who pretend to be what they're not. Absolutely no understanding of major emotions like shame, thinks everyone should be proud of his heritage without ever having been put to the test. Would Langley feel proud if her heritage were worn shopping bags and bunions and bubela babies? Old Langley should be shipped off to the Yeshiva to fill in the gaps in her own education, but I don't think that likely, so had better return to her home territory, the Andrews School (called "Andrews" by all in the know).*

First the place itself. Forget the schools you and I have known. Replace those iron steps that we used to troop up with red carpeting. Get out from the stairwells with their chicken-coop glass that tunneled us along and lightly embrace a swirling white bannister. Whatever you do, don't rush, because no one does. It isn't nice or proper or even necessary, because there are no crowds in private schools, and no one is going to trip you or walk over you or do anything noticeably not nice. Now let go of the bannister altogether because we're heading for the library, where a little bird named Miss Finch hangs out. On the way we pass Miss Millet, the school secretary, who lives in a closet that she has converted into an office.

The library was once the dining room, and Miss Finch, the librarian, watches over the rare books—"few though they may be; all donations from our ever grateful alumnae"—which rest on the shelves that once held fine china. (Are you getting the picture that everyone lives in a former something?) The library was painted white now and reminded me of a Christian Science Reading Room. When I looked in (on Miss Millet's advice) Miss Finch assumed I was a prospective student and immediately broke into the tour.

"Here's the required reading shelf, there's the suggested reading shelf. And by the door the shelf for the topic of the month is currently unoccupied, because the committee who decides such matters could not reach a decision." Fortunately the brief rundown exhausted Miss Finch and I was able to get away.

The big challenge is to get past Miss Langley's office and not be seen, for although the room (the real library once upon a time) is old and formal, Miss Langley has managed to add a touch of modernity by concealing the latest radar equipment behind all that wonderful wooden paneling, which is the only way she could know you are there even when she doesn't see you. Anyway, the room and Miss Langley set the tone for the school—traditional, confident, polite, and terrifying. Langley is pure blue-blood all the way 'round the circulatory system, but she has this partner, Tooley, her co-headmistress, who is short and stout and is stuffed into the back of the school, the former kitchen, where she attends to the rising cost of tuition and getting the girls into good colleges. Tooley sits with a tight ribbon binding her neck on which her Phi Beta Kappa key hangs. I don't know why she's willing to risk strangula-

tion. She seems like a cheerful buffoon type, and she together with Langley form a balanced slate. Langley, from old New York society, presents the front to the parents and incoming students while Tooley, pure Midwestern corn, gets them out and placed properly so Andrews can carry on.

Naturally it was Langley who interviewed me for the job. Only someone with great social confidence could risk hiring the first faculty Jew!

A few minutes ago I walked down a narrow flight of stairs undoubtedly designed to punish servants and opened the first door I saw, which turned out to be the students' dining room, where the conference was to be held. Three ladies in black uniforms and white aprons, who had undoubtedly just retired from Schraffts, dropped their doilies and jumped.

"Good Lord," said the first, "is it time yet?"

"Dearie me, are we late?" said the second.

"No, no," I answered just in time to catch the third, who then thanked the Lord that I was just looking. I left the ladies alone with the Lord and looked for a corner where I could hide. (Why are the Irish so much more frightened of the Lord than you seem to be?)

Anyway, I was now alone in the faculty room, where there are lounge chairs in the middle and work desks lined up against the wall like consciences in case someone might get comfortable. Ah, Canelli, do you think I am going to last here? (Teacher I'm replacing had a nervous breakdown, but Langley thought she sensed strong material.) The whole place makes me giddy. It doesn't seem real. My only hope of surviving is you. Can I smuggle out my secret thoughts whenever I'm about to go mad?

.ANDREWS.

The meeting is due to begin shortly and I must prepare to take my vows and be formally united to Andrews. Will continue later to tell you if I made it through the ceremony. If you don't hear from me, contact Bellevue.

Saturday morn
Have escaped from Andrews sanity intact. Miss Langley said as we parted for the weekend that she hoped some of the Andrews spirit would linger with me. It has, just like a hangover.

Weekly conferences are held, it seems with all the regularity of good bowel movements. But once they begin, a constant flow of irrelevancies interrupt proceedings and give the entire meeting a rhythm of polite insanity. . . .

———◄◆►———

"Well, Miss Frankfort, I hope you're all set to meet your colleagues. Why don't you take this chair next to me?"

First Miss Langley eyed the teacher in charge of tea, and when Mrs. Smith had pushed the silver samovar away from her, Langley commenced the meeting with a nod of her head as if she were cueing in a symphony orchestra.

"There we are, very good, I think we can now begin. Ladies and gentle*man,* before we start the official business of the day. . . ." Then Tooley at the opposite end lost her glasses. Langley, in the meantime, took three white triangles from the sandwich tray and a sprig of parsley before beginning all over again. Miss Millet sat off to the side and picked up her pencil, and I took one triangle from the sandwich tray. By the fourth official beginning I was still chewing my one sandwich, worried now whether I had digested my tongue as well. The insides of the sandwiches were filled with spreads so thin I began to think they were intentionally designed to cut down on noise.

Finally Langley got around to it. ". . . I have a most pleasurable task to perform. And probably a surprising one for those who are wondering why I have invited a pupil to our conference. No, it is not a pupil, contrary to appearance, whom I wish to introduce but our newest faculty member, Miss Frankfort. And although she is unquestionably our youngest staff member, Miss Frankfort does not come to us without some teaching experience behind her."

Quickly nostalgia turned into shame as Langley announced I came with teaching experience behind me—which she had the good sense to leave behind. I continued chewing. Now everything was really ready—parsley sprigs, lemon wedges, silver samovar of tea. First a bit of a sandwich and then a morsel of gossip about the daughter of a celebrity who is having a hard time because the family life is so messy. Pity, pity, pity, crunch, crunch, crunch. But not too noisy please, we're starting again.

"And now, having introduced Miss Frankfort, who will assume her teaching duties officially on Monday, I think the meeting can begin. Katherine," she turned to Miss Tooley; "will you announce the agenda for today?"

"Certainly, Agatha, but before we get down to business, I think we should get our tea. Are you ready to pour, Mrs. Smith?"

"Indeed, I am. Who would like tea today? How about you, Miss Frankfort, may I pour you a cup? What a pleasure, another tea drinker. Beatrice, please pass this around. As soon as I pour myself a cup, I'll hand the meeting back over to you, Katherine."

"Wait, Florence, I do believe I have on the wrong pair of glasses. However, let us carry on. I think I can manage. Here we are. Item number one. Should Andrews girls be allowed to drink their cokes through a straw in the bottle or should they continue to pour their cokes into glasses as has always been done? Discussion to precede vote. Two. What is to be done about Vicki Rose? Discussion. No vote. Three. How to proceed with plans for the mother-daughter luncheon to be held in the Spring. Discussion if time permits. Are there any questions? No? Objections? No? Good. Then let's start with item number one. Is there anyone to second that motion?"

"I do."

"Motion is seconded. Who will speak first?"

Mrs. Smith cleared her throat. "I will if I may. Now I know well that times are changing, and I know also all about young people and their need to keep up with the times. Some of the changes I even support. But there are limits, I maintain. Not for myself as much as for the girls. We are doing them no service by indiscriminately allowing them to go along with the times. Which is the point I wish to make. We cannot accept change for change's sake. I think for us to allow our girls to do away with the lovely habit of pouring soda into a glass would compromise not only us and them but the entire Andrews tradition."

"Thank you, Mrs. Smith. Let us hear some other opinions. Are there any among us who would wish to disagree with Mrs. Smith? Go ahead, Mrs. Bollinger."

"All I can do is thank God that we were not entrusted with

decision-making powers earlier in the century. For where would we be if we took a stand in favor of tradition. I say bosh to tradition . . ."

"That's because you're British, Sybil, and can say bosh to anything."

"Please, ladies, let Mrs. Bollinger finish."

"I still say bosh to tradition and hurray for progress. Let us look ahead, not behind. I want it known that I cast my vote for bottles and straws. And if it comes to a pinch, I will drink straight from a bottle without the straw!"

"May I make a point?"

"The floor is yours, Miss Finch."

"I do not know that it will further clarify matters but it seems to me that we have lost sight of a most fundamental issue. Is it *pretty* for a young lady to drink from a bottle, even *with* a straw? I mean does it look ladylike? After all, part of the education of our girls, I think we do all agree on this but of course I am open to correction if this be not so, is to teach them how to behave in a ladylike manner. I just do not think it *becomes* young ladies to drink from bottles. Which is all I have to say."

"Go ahead, Lee. Now you may speak."

"It just struck me right now that we should abolish soft drinks altogether and end the argument."

"What would you do, Lee, introduce hard liquor in its place?"

"Sybil, I'm being serious."

"The brevity of your proposal makes it hard to fully evaluate your position, Lee. I see Agatha has something to say."

"Thank you, Katherine. I too regret the passing of the days when gentility was considered a virtue, but *I* for one consider practicality no less a virtue than gentility. The time and cost saved by doing away with glasses are not to be minimized. If *I* were deciding things, there is no question in *my* mind about what would be done. Of course, I am *not* running things. I cast only one vote, and therefore cannot insist, only strongly urge, the rest of you to consider what to me are the very clear advantages of bottles. Now let us proceed with the vote."

We did. . . .

"Yes, Mrs. Smith, what is the outcome?"

"I am still counting, Miss Langley, but it looks to me as if bottles are ahead. Are all the slips in? Then let me total things. Well, won't you be surprised everyone, the new has triumphed over the old and glasses are to be replaced by bottles henceforth."

"We can't argue with democracy, so let us get along with the next topic, Florence."

"I too, Agatha, am anxious to proceed with topic two but first a word of apology to our sole gentleman member, Mr. McMann. I do hope our greatly admired art teacher will suffer no embarrassment. . . ."

The "sole gentleman faculty member," I later found out, married a former student with lots of money, who bought him a brownstone next to Andrews, where he conducts his art classes. His name was John McMann. He had thick and coarse hair, brownish sprinkled with the sandy gray hue that contemporary homes imitate when they go organic. But John McMann's features were far from earthy. He had a cultivated face which might have initially been rough but which the money from his Andrews marriage had softened. The only relic left of his Irish ancestry was a nose which was now small and perfect but looked filled with potential for becoming porcine. I thought the potential would be realized in a few years when his other features got fleshy with alcohol (they were now only a bit red) and his whole face blossomed into purple like lilacs after a spring rain.

"I don't think we have to worry, Florence, about John. He doesn't suffer embarrassment so easily. Let us get on with the topic."

"All right, Agatha. I shall not apologize anymore for calling attention to the pointiness of Vicki Rose's undergarment."

"Which one, Florence?"

"The one on top."

"Her brassiere, right?"

"Yes, Agatha, and the way she showed it off when she strutted across the stage during the school play. Do you have something to add, Beatrice?"

"Although I too thought I observed a slightly more pronounced thrust just at the moment Victoria stepped into focus, I think our indebtedness to Christian Charity should make us consider the possibility that the spotlights distorted our vision."

"Ladies and gentleman, I think we shall have to stop here. Why don't you, Florence, and all interested others form a committee to work out some satisfactory solution and present your findings next Friday at one."

"Pardon, Miss Langley, but I haven't read the minutes from last week yet."

"That too will have to wait until next Friday, Miss Millet. I like meetings to begin and to end on time. Now, Miss Frankfort, that you have met our faculty, I should imagine you'll be more at ease on Monday. We wouldn't want anyone staring at you as if you did not belong on your first day. Besides, being slowly eased into position is more comfortable then plunging right in. Not that there aren't times when a cold plunge is appropriate. But now you will have the entire weekend to grow accustomed to us. Of course, I don't expect you to spend all your time dwelling on Andrews. Goodness knows, teachers need their private lives too. But hopefully, something of our spirit will linger and make you more at home Monday. I look forward to seeing you then as well as future Fridays one o'clock sharp. As you see, there is always more to cover than time permits, and consequently our meetings are punctual. Although some of our members are not."

"Ellen, why don't you meet us for lunch, Monday?"

"I'm glad you didn't disappear Lee, I wanted to say good-bye to you."

"Don't bother. Just come down to the faculty room if you're free Monday."

"What time?"

"Eleven thirty is good. You can meet Claudine then. She wasn't here today. I think you'll get on."

"Fine. Now I must go see Miss Millet."

"If you start falling asleep, just start counting the number of times she ends a sentence with 'shall-we-say'."

"Here you are, Miss Frankfort, just in time. I have prepared a package of uh, homework, shall we say. (One) Why don't we go up to your room where we can spread out. It's up a flight on the second floor."

"My goodness, is this it? I never dreamed of having a real fireplace in my classroom."

"We don't use the ones in the classrooms any more but it once was a real fireplace."

"Just having it here is inspiring, even if it's not used."

"Good. Our girls can always use inspiration. Now as to the materials. It might be helpful for you to look at these. They are the last assignments Miss Hillson ever handed in. I've had some copies made up for you to take home and look over at your leisure. Of course, you needn't follow Miss Hillson. It is up to each individual teacher to decide how much and what kind of homework to give the girls. The only thing we demand is that by Wednesday of each week, if possible, but surely no later than Thursday—all our faculty submit daily homework assignments for the following week. That way, if someone is sick, there is a record of what material is being covered when the home calls, and we—that is, I do not have to bother you. Oh yes, attendance. That is mostly my affair. If a girl is not able to attend school she is expected to contact me first. I then inform you of her absence and the reason for it. If you note a girl's absence and do not hear from me by, let me see, midday, shall we say, (Two) I would appreciate your calling it to my attention. We don't of course have a problem with delinquency here, but every now and then there is a misunderstanding, shall we say.

(Three)

"Oh yes, another thing. Reading lists. I have given you one for each class and a set of books, your own, as well as the list of suggested reading from which the girls choose books for their monthly reports. We try to coordinate these things with our library, but since our collection is not unlimited, should you wish to assign a book that is not in our library you might speak to me first. I sometimes can suggest that we buy it. Of course, the Library Committee must meet and approve my suggestion, which can take a while. Often I find that the girls prefer paperbacks, which we buy wholesale as a saving for the parents. If the book is not too expensive, the girls often buy it with their own money—that is, their allowance—which by the way is usually too much, so don't hesitate to ask them to buy a book if you do not want to wait for the office to order it.

"And now I just thought of another thing, supplies. The girls are all expected to use standard paper which we provide. There is one kind for book reports, another for math, and so forth. We find that this kind of uniformity is very helpful in training girls to acquire orderly habits. Hence, we would appreciate it if you accept *only* standard paper. You do understand, I hope."

"Uh, yes."

"We do not want to inspire waste, so we give the girls a poorer quality of paper for scrap work of any kind. That is, we would not like to see girls using the best quality paper for, uh, rough drafts, shall we say. (Four) Likewise with school pencils which have Andrews written on them and are of a standard size lead. The girls do own their books, but nevertheless we discourage writing in them since we think it wise to instill a respect for possessions at the earliest age possible. I think, Miss Frankfort, that covers all I have to say. Here is the envelope with samples of what I've described. I see you are looking at the desk calendar."

"I was just turning it several weeks so it would be up to date on Monday."

"It, of course, belonged to Miss Hillson. I've given you a new one just for the sake of, uh, starting out clean, shall we say."

"Five."

"Five what?"

"No, no, I was just thinking, six, six, weeks more . . ."

"I know, and it will be vacation time. No need to blush. We all look forward to vacations here. We work hard when we work and then try to recover when we don't."

"Do you have any questions you might like to ask me before we leave?"

"I was just wondering where the girls are on Friday afternoons."

"The girls get half a day off on Fridays. They often have to get to their country homes or hairdressers or whatever and it works out well. They do what they have to and we have our meetings without them."

"I see."

"If there are no further questions I'll say goodbye to you now and shall look forward to seeing you Monday. If anything puzzling turns up please feel free to call on me."

"Thank you, Miss Millet. Have a nice weekend."

A stickler for fine print, I made my way through the Andrews reading list, the Andrews *suggested* reading list, and the Andrews catalogue. It was printed right there in the catalogue. Andrews wasn't Andrews when it was first founded.

Andrews used to be called the Goldschmidt School for Girls "because in the late eighteen hundreds and early nineteen hundreds, young women of Jewish origin had a hard time gaining admission to the best private schools and not being satisfied with inferior educational institutions decided to found one themselves." Once the Guggenheims and Lehmanns were no longer barred from the top schools, they left their places at Goldschmidt for the nouveau riches to inherit. I'm sure the Guggenheims and Lehmanns did not have an all-Christian faculty or hire Agatha B. Langley to run their school. If they had all that money, they weren't that insecure. Just proud that they were shrewd enough to get a dame whose family had always run America.

The whole thing with Langley was she could combine impeccable politeness with sheer terror. And of course, she had no notion of shame. But then, neither would you if your father and all his forefathers were running the country and you sailed through Miss Chapins, Vassar and the Atlantic as if there were no other route for young women to take. That's what Langley had to offer: her confidence.

Monday morning I arrived punctual as a point all prepared "to officially assume my teaching duties," as Miss Langley, who greeted me, put it. Once again I was to be escorted, this time to my class, and had I been a little less uncomfortable I might have felt like a visiting dignitary.

"I'm sure Miss Millet explained that your homeroom class is the First Senior Form. We call them the Senior I's for convenience. In addition to them, you'll have the Senior II's and III's for English. They should present no problem at all, but something seems to have happened to our Senior I's. Mrs. Smith insists they were a fine group when they first started out as Junior I's and were still okay even as Junior II's. There are only fifteen in the class, but they are a clever little crew with an average I.Q. of 134. Unfortunately their brains are not worth a farthing when it comes to matters of self-control. But I am confident you'll be able to handle them instead of the reverse, as was the case, I'm afraid, with poor Annie Hillson."

"Some of the terminology confuses me. I'm not sure of the difference between the Juniors and Seniors."

"I assumed you knew that. Junior I is the first grade of our upper school, the equivalent of a seventh-grade elementary class. Junior II's are eighth grade, and then when they start the high school years we call them Seniors, starting of course with the First Senior Form which we call the Senior I's. They are your homeroom class, and you will teach them English and grammar. The girls have some sort of aversion to grammar this year, so we've segregated it from the rest of the English program and given it a separate name. It's now called "General Language" and meets at a different time from English. Instead of devoting part of each lesson to grammar the way Miss Hillson did, we are limiting it to two lessons a week. Twice should suffice if you can control the girls. What do you say to that?"

"Very sensible indeed."

"Good. I would not want our girls to go through Andrews without learning grammar. There are certain basic skills, and grammar is one. I don't care how you do it as long as you get the job done. And manage to remain sane yourself. Andrews cannot afford another breakdown."

Miss Langley looked at me once to check my condition before we proceeded up the flight of stairs. I stared straight back at her because that is what confident people do. She drew in her chest and turned her face so that one jaw was more prominent than the other. When we arrived at the classroom all the girls stood up.

"No occasion for formality, ladies." Miss Langley made a quick motion as if she was brushing a fly from her sleeve and the class sat down. "I am not here on an official tour of duty. I have come with a pleasurable task, that of presenting to you your new teacher, and I am sure that she will handle whatever ceremony is fitting. But let me warn you. I strongly suspect your new teacher will not stand for any *unnecessary* ceremony. Here, then, is Miss Frankfort."

Miss Langley wasted no time in leaving, but her presence lingered like a strong disinfectant and the girls sat stiffly at attention.

"Where shall we begin?"

No response.

"How about someone telling me what you have been doing in English up until now. Yes, the girl with the long blonde hair."

"I was just pushing my hair behind my ears, Miss Frankfort."

"Sorry, does anyone else want to speak? I think we're a small enough group so that you don't have to raise your hand. You can speak out."

"You may be sorry about that, Miss Frankfort."

"Why?"

"Well, we used to do that with the teacher who was here before."

"Miss Hillson?"

"Yes. And she didn't like us too much."

"How come?"

"To tell the truth, Miss Frankfort, we were not very nice to her."

"It's hard to be nice to someone who doesn't like you. Don't you think?"

"No, I mean the reason she didn't like us is because we were not nice to her. It really was *our* fault."

"Well, you can't be that nasty if you admit your faults so readily."

That did it. The girls responded as if I had given an "at ease."

"How about the work? What were you reading? The girl in the back with the beige sweater. Did you want to talk?"

"No, I mean I didn't want to answer your question. I wanted to ask you something else."

"Go ahead."

"What I really wanted to ask you, Miss Frankfort, was, um . . . do you know how Miss Hillson is? I mean did she have to go to a . . . an institution?"

"I don't know. Perhaps Miss Langley does."

"Egads. We could never ask Miss Langley. We just couldn't."

"I think I understand. Miss Langley *is* a very formidable being."

"A what being?"

"A *formidable* being. What do you think it means? Well, what are Miss Langley's characteristics?"

"Scary."

"Big."

"Okay. How about impressive, overwhelming, inspiring some awe?" I stood up and wrote the word on the blackboard. "Now let's get back to the work. What books were you reading?"

"This awful grammar book," a girl in the back said.

I looked at the textbook she held up. "Surely you weren't *reading* that. I mean, what literature were you reading?"

"*Victor of Salamis,* Miss Frankfort. Do you like it?"

"I've never heard of it. What is it about?"

"Well, it's this big long thing about a war. The reason we read it is because it fits in with Mrs. Smith's history class. Actually, she decides what we read, not the English teacher. And she likes us to read books that tie in with what she teaches."

"Miss Frankfort, are you going to have us write a book report each month?"

"And are you going to let us use the same report for English as we write for History? Miss Hillson did."

"Hold it, girls. Offhand I'd say that I'd like to select the books you read, but I must find out how much I'm free to change things."

"Miss Frankfort, why is it necessary to write book reports?"

"Hmm. A good question. I don't really know why English teachers act as if students can't survive without them. Probably we're afraid students won't read the assignments unless they have to write a report."

"That means you don't trust us then," said a girl with an old-fashioned middy blouse.

"Let's see. How many of you feel you would not read the book unless you had to write a book report?"

I was astounded. Almost all the hands went up.

"You seem so honest *now* it's hard to believe you'd lie about your reading. Don't you like to read, or is it the particular books you don't like?"

"Both," several girls said in unison.

"Let me see what I can do to change the reading list for a start and to think of some alternative way of checking up on you besides book reports. How do you feel about keeping a journal as you read?"

"What would we put in it?"

"You could keep track of all the passages that excited you one way or the other, and jot down characters whom you liked or hated. And then when you were all finished you could look over your notes and try to figure out why you reacted strongly."

"That sounds like fun."

"It's more fun than writing a book report, and what's more, I can check upon you with greater accuracy. A journal is impossible to copy. No two people can have the same strong responses and the same reasons for those responses, so you can't copy from each other. And also, you can't go to a trot and read a summary of a plot and then put it into your own words."

"Miss Frankfort, you must have been teaching for a long time. You know so much about cheating."

"Don't you think *I* ever cheated? What's the name of the girl who just spoke? Patti? Well, anyway, if you keep a book journal I'll have a chance to get to know you, and you'll also have a chance to learn more about yourselves. Just like when you write a diary. Yes, what is it?"

"I think it's past the hour."

I looked at my watch. "You're right. What is your next class?"

"Art."

"We had better stop right now. Don't you have to go over to the next building for that?"

"Yes, the Studio. That's what Mr. McMann likes us to call his house."

"Jody, you forgot to tell Miss Frankfort that Mr. McMann doesn't care if we're late."

"That's true. Mr. McMann says it's silly to worry about lateness because art is timeless."

After all the girls had disappeared down the staircase, I closed my door and left for the faculty lounge. Two teachers were sitting on lounge chairs. I recognized Lee from the faculty meeting. The other face was unfamiliar.

"Come in and join us, Ellen. I don't think you've met Claudine."

"No, I haven't."

Claudine said nothing until I sat down. Then without moving any other part of her body, she turned her face toward me, caught my eyes, and looked directly at me. A quick quiver passed below her cheekbone. "Hello," she said. "Are you new here?"

"That's right. You weren't here Friday. I should have told

you Ellen is taking Annie's place in the English Department."

"I'm not sure Annie's completely gone. The place is haunted with her memory."

"The whole thing was so unfortunate."

"Tell me, was she small?"

"Annie? God, no. She was big boned and looked stronger than any of us. You know, the ones you least expect."

"How funny. I have this image of little Annie Hillson, fragile and nervous."

"Oh, Annie was always a bit mad, but in the best way. Wouldn't you agree?"

Claudine flicked her cigarette. "You know how I feel about discussing this, Lee."

"Come off it, Claudine. You like gossip as much as anyone."

"Only in bed." Claudine put out her cigarette slowly until there was nothing left to crush. "How are your classes, Ellen. Have you had any yet?"

"I met my homeroom class, the Junior—no the Senior I's —and they seem fine."

"The best thing would be if you could like them," Lee said, turning her whole body around in the chair so that she now faced me instead of Claudine. "Annie was really contemptuous of them."

"They seem to know that. Why did she feel that way?"

"Because they're not really intellectual, and Annie was. They're mainly interested in fashions and boys and Annie wasn't."

"Sounds just like the kids I went to school with."

"Which one was that?"

"A public high school where the kids, the parents, and even the teachers except for the couple of spinsters still around, were like that. Real rah rah."

"Then you'll probably do well here. One difference, though. These kids are fantastically spoiled. They have a lot of money, and no one knows what to do with it. The other difference is that the faculty, for the most part, is typical private school stuff, so you have all sorts of cultural clashes."

"Not cultural, Lee. Just clashes of class."

"What do you teach, Claudine?"

"Languages, mainly French and one class of Spanish."

"So you can talk about bullfighting, Claudine, admit it," Lee said, turning back to face Claudine.

"No, it's not true."

"Then why do my girls always write English compositions about your going off to Spain and having wild affairs with bullfighters?"

"Probably because of your lectures on Hemingway."

"Do you lecture on Hemingway, Lee? The little I saw of reading lists and books made me skeptical about literary taste at Andrews."

"That's because of Mrs. Smith. She's the closest this school comes to medievalism. The *worst* of the private school tradition—narrow, self-righteous, and completely lacking any sense of style or concern for esthetics. A horrible old moralist who's constantly titillated by the immoral."

"Why do they put up with her if she's so bad?"

"She's been around a long time. Everyone has to pay homage to her as if she's some ancient institution on the verge of demise. She *is*, except she never demises. Half your time will be spent undoing what she's done. I'd better shut up, someone is at the door."

"Good morning, ladies," Miss Langley said, landing hard on the "morning." "I just thought I might find you here, Miss Grenier," she said to Claudine. "It was on your account that I had some rather unpleasant tasks this summer, and it all can be traced to something you said. I should not have been told it before vacation. That gave me an entire summer to think about it."

Claudine sat quietly with her eyes resting on Miss Langley's tall frame.

"Let me remind you of the remark. If memory serves me correctly, it was you, Miss Grenier, who informed me that the elderberry jelly I made for the cake sale was the best you ever tasted, and when I thought of your comment this summer, I felt compelled to make some more even though *I* use store-bought jelly myself. In return for your disclosure, I have left a jar of jelly with Miss Millet. You can pick it up whenever you like. Good day."

"Isn't she marvelous," Claudine said when the door closed. "Who else can present a gift as a grand accusation?"

"I'm glad you appreciate it. I might have passed out if I were in your position."

"You get used to it, Ellen, and actually it becomes charming. Especially if you have a flair for the sadistic. Miss Langley is far too sensitive socially to criticize a teacher in front of others. I knew right away that she was about to compliment me or give me a gift."

"That's because of your intuitive grasp of the sadistic, Claudine."

"Perhaps. I think I'll go get the jelly now so we can have it for lunch."

Lee and I left the lounge and went into the student cafeteria. There I was introduced to Theresa, Maureen, and Mary.

"They're the three ladies in black who served at the conference, aren't they?"

"Yes, and they'll bring a tray into the faculty lounge if you tell them what you want. I do hope you like gourmet dishes like hashed leftover meat patties and potatoes," Lee whispered. "It's their specialty."

I could see why Claudine went for the elderberry jelly.

"Mary, can you put some extra bread on the tray today, please? And three specials. What's today's? Tuna pie? Is that all right with you, Ellen? Yes, Mary, you can make it three, please. We'll be in the lounge," Lee called out.

"I swear that tuna pie is from Friday's tuna salad. I don't know why I'm complaining. Actually, you get used to the food after a while, like everything else here."

"Miss Frankfort, could I have a few minutes with you alone? Are you free now?"

"Of course, Mrs. Smith, come in." I pulled a chair over from the center of the room, and down she sat.

"I see you prefer a circular seating arrangement to the standard one of rows."

"Yes, it seems more conducive to informal discussions. Everyone can see all the faces, not just the backs of heads. I think students get bored less easily when they talk to everyone, not just to me."

"I see. I always thought that boredom had more to do with the lesson, but I could be mistaken. However, there are a few things I feel confident about. You must understand, Miss Frankfort, I am an old-timer here, and have seen many girls come and go. They are all for the most part nice young ladies, and I am proud of them. But something does happen at about 13, the age of your Senior I's, which if allowed to go unchecked could have unfortunate results. I need not tell you that this is the time they become boy crazy. Even the best of them. If this is encouraged or even left on its own, they will learn nothing. It is precisely for this reason that I drew up a reading list devoid of romantic content except on the noblest level. I need not add that the revisions you made came as a shock."

"I'd be delighted to talk about them."

"Between you and me, Miss Frankfort, there are some Senior III's, not even IV's, mind you, who know more about life than either you or I." Mrs. Smith lowered her voice. "And I am a married woman," she said in a confessional tone, "with two daughters and five grandchildren."

Mrs. Smith paused to catch her breath. When she resumed her composure, her color had not fully returned and there was a vague glint of blue in her face like the one in the pearls she was fingering.

"I don't *really* object to *Huckleberry Finn,* although I might have picked *Tom Sawyer* myself. He's always seemed like a nicer sort to me. But Holden Caulfield is a disgraceful child, and I'm concerned about having the girls read *Catcher in the Rye.* And I know that youngsters will read books like that on the sneak, so to speak. The devil always has an advantage over the angels when it comes to the young. All I question is whether we should make his lot any easier."

"I hadn't really thought of myself as being in collusion with the devil."

"But when girls are going through a stage of life when their morals are being shaped, don't you think everything must be thought of in those terms?"

"Yes, but I also think I'd like to train them to be sensitive to matters of style and form."

"What is wrong with the style of *Victor of Salamis?* The grammar sets a far better example than that in *Catcher in the Rye.* I shan't even *compare* the vocabulary."

"But the girls don't find the book interesting."

"Must a book always be interesting? Isn't the fact that it is instructive enough? I think, Miss Frankfort, that a *good* teacher can stimulate interest in the dullest bit of work. It is my firm conviction, based on years of experience, that pupils are by nature lazy. There is going to be resistance to anything that isn't strictly trash."

"Would it be feasible for the girls to read both the books you recommend and the ones I do?"

"Feasible, but hardly fair. After all, they do have subjects that require a lot of work, and I have always had an arrangement with the English teacher that we help the girls out. The English teacher has always permitted the girls to use for their English book reports what they submit to me for their history reports—which are absolutely mandatory, always have been and will be. Which brings me to my next point. How can you possibly consider a personal journal an improvement over the book report?"

"I don't think that girls so young have the ability to review a book. Literary criticism is a very difficult skill, and since the girls can't possibly have developed it at their age, all they can do is retell the story, which doesn't seem like an educational exercise for anyone."

"Our points of view are so terribly apart that I don't see how we can discuss it. I'll just ask you about one other change —your substituting 'Romeo and Juliet' for 'Merchant of Venice'."

"The girls are first starting to read Shakespeare seriously, and I think it would aid their learning if they started out with a play they enjoy. You said that they think of nothing but boys, so why not capitalize on some of that interest and use it for motivation?"

"Perhaps, Miss Frankfort, we might do better to discuss this all with a third disinterested party, like Miss Langley."

Sunday

Father Confessor Canelli,

Andrews has moved from coke bottles to broader points, and I have triumphed in my first battle. Victory came at a private conference held in Langley's office.

First, the setting: Langley, Mrs. Smith, and I were all seated politely, ankles crossed, thighs unexposed, in captains' chairs. Grandfather clock watched over us in the corner and all was very cozy. But Mrs. Smith was not happy. She was "a bit concerned over some curriculum changes made by the newest member of our faculty. Let us begin with the matter of book reports."

I still remember what a drag they were to write and how if you summarized the story the teacher would say, "If I wanted to find out what the book was about, I could have read Dickens myself who knows the story better than you."

Mrs. Smith, who got very nervous when she heard the word "journal" or "diary," immediately thought of the personal, which, as we all know is only one hot breath away from the immoral. Langley, clever lady that she was, diagnosed the problem right away. "Why don't we call the journal the Revised Book Report?" Mrs. Smith was forced to capitulate. So much for victory one. Onward to the next battle—the choice of books. I replaced Mrs. Smith's historical novel with Huckleberry Finn. *This time Mrs. Smith was right to protest, although naturally she objected for the wrong reasons.* Huckleberry Finn *does a fine job of attacking prissy hypocrites like her. He even can serve as a model for revolt—leaving home, declaring independence from the Mrs. Smiths, and recognizing their phoniness. Holden Caulfield helps Huckleberry out when it comes to showing that young people are purer, in general, than adults. Of course, Mrs. Smith could not object to* Huckleberry Finn *because it's a classic. To Langley I argued that I can teach only those books which I believe in, and by exploiting her vulnerability for self-reliance, Langley went along with me here too.*

The interruptions in meetings are like good TV commercials—more entertaining than the show. Miss Millet announced that Dotty and Marie had arrived.

"Invite them in, please," said Langley. The door opened

and in strutted two females in tight pants, one in cerise and the other in chartreuse. Through their sweaters two tiny juts protruded. Both had bleached hair which was barely visible behind the armies of bobby pins surrounding their heads. Not only were they missing real breasts, but they lacked eyebrows as well. Instead, two mechanical marks streaked across their foreheads.

Miss Langley stood up and in the very manner used to greet trustees at the annual fund-raising dinner she extended her hand and said, "How do you do, Dotty. I'm so glad to see you, Marie. Won't you please have a seat."

Langley winked at Mrs. Smith and myself, and we abdicated our chairs. I recognized Dotty and Marie as the pair who had been jeering at Andrews girls after school. Finch had told our girls not to look at Dotty and Marie so that they wouldn't feel different, but Dotty and Marie refused to stop hanging around. Miss Langley decided to chat with them before resorting to the police. Dotty exchanged a confused look with Marie, and Mrs. Smith and I exited. I don't know what happened within those paneled walls, but Dotty and Marie have not been seen since their fireside chat with Miss Langley.

We all resumed our seats. Fortunately, Langley realized that morality goes beyond issues of necking and petting and was not put off by plays about love. So Huck Finn, Romeo, Juliet, and even Holden Caulfield were permitted to stay, and I was on my way to another victory when we took time out for interruption number two.

Lucy, a Senior III, was about to enter. Evidently Lucy had been seen going up to a boy's apartment after school and hung about a corner hamburger joint where non-Andrews types congregated. Mrs. Smith, self-appointed deputy chief of morality, offered to pass by daily to see where Lucy went after school. But Langley would have nothing to do with spying. In came Lucy looking calm and self-confident.

Langley motioned for her to sit down, and then in the sweetest tone: "Well, Lucy, how are you enjoying sexual intercourse these days?"

Lucy burst into tears, Mrs. Smith nearly slipped off her chair, and Langley told Lucy to go quiet herself in the ladies' room. "You see, Florence, I do not believe in being indirect. Call an act by its correct name and you are more likely to get a reliable response. Which reminds me, Miss Frankfort, I'd like to ask you a question." Mrs. Smith, sensing the worst, excused herself and I was left alone with Langley.

"Miss Frankfort, some of the girls are requesting half a day off for the Jewish holiday next week, and I'd like to know how important a holiday it is."

"I can't really say," I told her. Langley was appalled. She had as much contempt for Jews who are ignorant of their religion as she did for young girls who had sexual intercourse. Ah, the old heritage business all over again.

<hr />

Lee, who had dropped by to borrow my hairdryer, pulled up a chair next to the desk where I was spread out with the creative compositions of the week.

" 'The reflecting pool answered me back with the same

empty stares thrown into it. There was no escaping the re-
flections.' My god, what did you assign them?"

" 'A Description of a Particular Place.' "

She went on reading as she stood over my shoulder, " 'I
threw a stone into it. The stone made ripples, one larger than
the other in circles and the circles began to resemble eyes.
The circles widened, then like life, began to fade.' Ellen,
are you depressing these children? Why is life fading for a
fifteen-year-old girl? I can't stand this phony sensitivity."

"Symbolism isn't easy for fifteen-year-olds, Lee. I must
tell Julie to start out assuming I *know* she's sensitive. Oh
God, she wants to get everything in. Listen to this, 'The ripples
faded and now the sun too was fading. Only I was left with
pools of thought, as deep as the ocean, but I could bear it
no longer, I now knew what I must do. Throw myself into
the water like the stone.'

"The stone did *not* throw itself into the water, Julie. And
how did the ocean get into the picture?"

"She was very restrained about the fading sun, though.
Don't be too rough."

"Now she has the sun disappearing behind a mountain. So
we have pools, oceans, mountains, sunsets. And here's a 'low
limitless horizon.' Which of course she can see perfectly behind the mountain as the ocean tide rolls in on the stones in
the pool. What are you going to say?"

"I've told her I *know* she is sensitive and to see me in a
private conference so we can discuss how to develop her
talents by the use of restraints. How's that? Kind enough?"

"Well, Ellen, the conference should make her feel good.

Only the very worst and the best are invited to those, if I remember correctly. Now what have we got?"

" 'The Room.' "

"That sounds defined. Let's just hope she doesn't hang herself in it."

"Miss Tooley and I have been thinking about you these last few days, Miss Frankfort, and we have reached certain conclusions. Katherine, why don't you present the account?"

"All right, Agatha. Miss Langley and I have not had a chance to observe your behavior formally."

"We should let Miss Frankfort know that it is not our philosophy to observe the faculty formally. We receive more than enough information on *every* aspect of a teacher's relations. Now do continue, Kate. I just thought it important we make that clear, so Miss Frankfort need not fear an inquisition."

"No, indeed. Once we accept someone here, we do not feel it necessary to investigate her any further, under ordinary circumstances. What's more, should she prove unsatisfactory —that is, not fitting in with the way of life here at Andrews —we find that out soon enough. Our little ladies are the fastest informers in the world, and word quickly gets back in the form of parental complaints. I sometimes feel the girls are more harsh in their judgments than we would be, should we elect to evaluate our faculty by observing classes in session."

"Let us return to the point, Katherine—the relationship of Miss Frankfort, in particular, to her girls."

"Yes. Your relationship, Miss Frankfort, to your girls

strikes us as a fine one. That is, the girls seem to respond to you and you to them."

"Kate, again you must pardon me, but I do think you omitted an essential point. They *respect* Miss Frankfort, which is what impresses *me*. It is easy to be liked but to win respect is a more challenging affair."

"Miss Langley is absolutely right. Even though Miss Langley and I reach our opinions completely independently, they almost always coincide."

"Now, on the basis of our independent opinions, we wish to make a proposal which you are by no means obligated to accept, of course. Miss Tooley and I think it a fine idea to have you chaperone the dance we are planning with Harrison, our brother school. Young people respond well to other young people, and we are convinced the girls would enjoy having you at their dance. Of course, Mrs. Smith has always been a chaperone, and we have no plans to change that. Mrs. Smith is excellent when it comes to protocol and, goodness knows, we could not do without her. There must be someone to handle the formal invitation to the headmaster and so on, for these affairs do require advance preparation. And when it comes to that, we allow Mrs. Smith the last word since she is so experienced. But we do feel it would be more balanced if the two of you were to take on the job. In other words, we are not asking you to burden yourself with the time-consuming formal details. What we would like to know is, are you willing to attend the dance and remain throughout?"

"I say fine. I've never chaperoned a dance before, but I'm willing to give it a try."

"That is the spirit we like. Katherine, I think we can congratulate ourselves on our choice, if I must say so myself."

"Indeed, Agatha, we are lucky to have Miss Frankfort with us. *I* knew it as soon as I saw her conducting a study hall the first week she arrived. I just happened to be pausing for breath, and her door was opened sufficiently for me to spot a girl who was not studying. Miss Frankfort walked over to the girl and told her that no one came to *her* study hall who did not intend to study. And then when the girl made no move, Miss Frankfort placed a book in front of her and said, 'If you choose to remain here but cannot contain yourself from drifting off into daydreams, you are to make a *pretense* of studying so that I am unaware you are doing anything else.' That did it. The girl opened her book, Miss Frankfort went back to her own work, and I gathered sufficient breath to resume my climb."

"Katherine, I'll never know why you must climb stairs at all with your ascending blood pressure."

"There are times when it is necessary to climb stairs, no matter what, Agatha."

"I can't agree with that, but I shall not pursue the point. Tell me, Miss Frankfort, will you come alone or will you have an escort?"

"Oh, do bring an escort if you'd like. Mrs. Smith always enjoys meeting the friends of our faculty."

"Of course, you needn't bring anyone," Miss Langley said. "Miss Frankfort may prefer to come alone, Katherine."

"Katherine, I do think you ought to mention *why* Mrs. Smith comes alone."

"Of course, of course. Mr. Smith is an invalid. Has been for quite some time, so it is perfectly natural that he stay home. Fortunately for us, it does not prevent Mrs. Smith from attending school functions, although she cannot get home too late."

"No one can, Kate. Certainly not our girls, and I am sure that Miss Frankfort does not want to stay at a school dance forever."

"No, not forever, although I'm curious to be there. It's a first experience for me. As far as an escort goes. . . ."

"Give yourself time to decide. I'm sure the dance will present no problems for you. Anyone who can handle the Senior I's can clearly take on boys a year older. Girls are much more difficult at 13 than are boys. As a matter of fact, one of the jobs you will have is to protect the boys from our girls. Girls can be terribly aggressive, and most of the boys just don't seem interested in them. I've always suspected that not a one would show up if the headmaster did not require it. What is a duty for some is a pleasure for others."

"If everything is settled, Agatha, we can give Florence the go-ahead signal to get the proceedings under way. We'll let you know the exact day of the dance as soon as we receive an answer, but I can assure you that it will not be for a month and that it will be held on a Friday evening."

Miss Langley looked at the grandfather clock. "Katherine, it is six o'clock. I think we have kept Miss Frankfort long enough."

Miss Tooley uncurled herself from the chair in which she sat and stood up next to Miss Langley.

"Thank you for staying so late, Miss Frankfort."

"*And* for consenting to chaperone the dance, Kate."

Before I left the school, I stopped to use a bathroom—my bladder could hold out no longer. The bathroom was part of a little lounge area that must have once been a powder room used by guests. In the mirror of the lounge I could see Miss Tooley standing next to Miss Langley, who hovered over her in the protective shadows of the heavy wooden doors. Miss Langley looked relaxed and called Miss Tooley "Katie." There was something in the scene that made me feel shy, as if I were intruding. I don't know. Maybe they were lovers, maybe not. The students speculated about their sex lives as frequently as their fathers speculated on the market. But I was not sure. All I knew was that there was a closeness that touched me. As I passed them, Miss Tooley waved and Miss Langley smiled. Tooley, silly and sentimental; Langley, proper and erect for the last pose of the day before the doors closed and they were alone to pull down the shades and shut out whatever light was able to penetrate the interior of the old brownstone house.

Monday

Oh, Canelli,

Guess whom I've been dancing with lately. Not one but fifteen young prep school boys. But don't despair; I haven't gone desperate and taken to young boys. I have merely been performing my professional duty chaperoning a wholly non-incestuous affair between sister and brother schools. So here goes another installment on the life for a day—only now it's a night—of a private school teacher followed by a short period of peace. But if peace comes, war can't be far behind, and Mrs. Smith and I are back fighting again.

First we had to prepare for the dance. The envelope for

the invitation to the headmaster of Harrison, our brother school, was personally licked by Mrs. Smith, who handles the protocol end. A decent interval of a week was granted for a reply. Harrison turned out to be more than decent, and in four days time told Mrs. Smith that the boys were pleased to accept an invitation to attend a dance at Andrews—at another time. The one proposed had already "been set aside for a sporting event." Old devil Smith smiled when informing the girls of the delay—a knowing smile based on one husband, two daughters, and five grandchildren.

"You see, girls, this is what it is going to be like. Having patience, putting up with delays, and learning not to push yourself on the opposite sex, who have many more things to think about besides you." Mrs. Smith likes delays, postponements, and having to compose another letter to the headmaster of Harrison. Three days later the second reply to the second invitation arrived and the date was set. "The girls can now go out and buy new dresses," Mrs. Smith announced with glee, as if each boy had individually responded to her. "But girls," she said, "do remember boys are funny creatures. They are not to be pushed, pressed, or pressured, even now that they are a year older than they've been in previous years." (A great concession to psychology had been made by inviting boys a year older than the girls, since all the experts say girls mature much faster than boys.) "Don't think one year more makes a great difference. It doesn't. Boys will be boys no matter how old, and you must learn the art of being young ladies if you are to be noticed at all."

Finally the Friday arrived and Mrs. Smith had some last

words of warning: "Dress simply and pat your lipstick with a tissue, for few things are more vulgar than greasy red lips. Beware of young men who go in for such things." (Pretty good advice, though she didn't realize it.) "Same for your shoes—no heel higher than an inch. If you disobey me, you will tower over the boys, and no decent young man will ask you to dance.

"We should allow at least half an hour for inspection. Lips are no problem," she said to me. "But the eyes. They are another matter. Watch out for the eyes," Mrs. Smith warned. "Even though the girls know they are not allowed to use eye makeup, some do. A few are so skillful it is hard to detect they have anything on. I once had a girl, a pale little thing, who came in with rouge all over her cheeks. By the time I finished with her she didn't need any. A good embarrassment will bring out more color than rouge.

"Half an hour must be allowed for removal of any excess makeup that would not be in keeping with the Andrews tradition." Red lips, black eyebrows all clash with Andrews colors, green and white. "Although it is not my place to tell a colleague what to wear, I thought it might be helpful for you to have some guidelines since this is your first dance." Mrs. Smith went on to suggest a simple dress, the kind you might wear to a concert. "Of course, you do want to get a little dressed up out of consideration for our girls. I don't imagine you would want to dress in the same manner as you do for teaching," she said, staring at my black turtle-necked top and my wraparound skirt with its leather material and animalistic associations. "A nice woolen dress with some

pearls, perhaps. Or any simple necklace will do. And it might be wise for you to come before the girls arrive." (Obviously, Mrs. Smith was allowing time to look me over too.) "There are all sorts of last minute things to do. There is one more question before we go. I do hope you will not think that I am prying into your personal life, for I do not believe in that, but I think it essential to know whether you have invited a beau to the dance." Neither Miss Langley nor Miss Tooley seemed certain on this point. "I am coming alone," I said with classic simplicity. Mrs. Smith looked upset. How could I deprive her of a chance to form the final judgment by meeting my "beau"? Fortunately, forming judgments was such a reflex for Mrs. Smith that she recovered from her disappointment and in a moment of candor said, "That makes two of us all alone. Mr. Smith cannot attend social affairs, so I too will be without an escort. But I am sure we can manage. No sense in worrying ourselves into a state of fatigue when we have been excused for the afternoon. I personally hate missing a Friday noon conference, but Miss Langley insists we get some rest before returning tonight."

At 7:00 P.M., two carriage lamps lit the Andrews entrance, and I stepped inside all anxious that I look good. But for whom? Mrs. Smith? "Our girls?" The yet unseen Harrison boys? Who knew? Mrs. Smith was already in the large gym room bedecked with ribbons and party paraphernalia. The Schrafft's ladies were busy setting up the refreshment table while Mrs. Smith decided where to place the punch bowl, how to spread out the potato chips and pretzels in a manner neither skimpy nor overly abundant. The borrowed strand of pearls I wore strictly for her went unnoticed amid so many important details.

"Good, Miss Frankfort, you are here. We can use some help right now. I think we should not put out all our goodies at once but keep some in reserve. Could you take these bags and place them in an inconspicuous spot in the locker room?'

Now the girls began to arrive, nervous and giggly, and Mrs. Smith tried to put them at ease. "Judith, that is a lovely dress. Anna, do you know a little thread is hanging here. Where is my scissors? Let me clip it off before any of our young men arrive. Quick, quick, get me my bag." Mrs. Smith was prepared for all emergencies. "Girls, girls, do not cluster. You will scare the boys away if you are all together. Spread yourselves out, look your sweetest, and don't be silly whatever you do. Ah, if only Mr. Smith could see you now. You all look so pretty, I wish I had a camera." Mrs. Smith was so excited she did not notice the underlined eyes, the painted lips, and the heels higher than an inch. By the time the boys were due, I don't think Mrs. Smith could see, so much time was spent winking her steel blue eyes and wrinkling her own heavily rouged cheeks as she stood around waiting for devilment—while admonishing everyone to be calm and sweet and above all, unobtrusive. I kept on fearing that she was going to put some girl in reserve with the pretzels and potato chips so as not to give everything away at once.

Now a girl went into the locker room to comb her hair for the fiftieth time, and Mrs. Smith followed. "The more you comb it the worse it gets," she said as if stating Newton's third law. "You look perfectly lovely as you are. Don't improve on God's gifts, Barbara, have confidence in yourself. Put that mirror away, Patti, that is a sure sign of lack *of confidence. Now out of the locker room, all of you. This room is for the boys to deposit their coats, and it would be totally inappropriate to have one of you here when they come. Don't just stand there, Anna. You must learn not to be obvious. Mystery, girls, mystery, and subtlety above all."*

Mrs. Smith was getting carried away. Even her hands were gaining color as her eyes darted about. "Now, what is that I hear?" And with the sound of footsteps on the stairs, Mrs. Smith shooed everyone out of the locker room as if cleaning out a chicken coop. "They are coming," she cried. "I am almost certain." At this point any sane person would have drawn a gun had he not known Mrs. Smith's hysteria was due to five young boys, all in blue blazers with school insignias.

Mrs. Smith winked at herself once in the mirror before promenading out to meet the contingent. "Welcome, boys, to Andrews. Let me show you where you are to put your wraps." They all followed Mrs. Smith into the locker room, though not one had a wrap. Then out they came, sticking together like an unevenly pasted puppet.

"Let me introduce myself and get to know your names, young men." The five now separated to shake hands with Mrs. Smith, but even as single entities they continued to move as automatons. The boys whispered their names and each extended a hand, thumbs perpendicular to the four other fingers, which went forward as one unit. Now another group

of seven arrived, bypassing Mrs. Smith for the five in the farthest corner of the room. The girls who had been trying to spread themselves apart closed ranks, and Mrs. Smith whispered, "We cannot allow this to happen." Then in a loud voice she asked, "Which one of you young men can help me with the record player?"

Three came over, one pressed down the button of the old portable player, and all returned to their corner.

"Miss Frankfort, I think you should try to intervene. Youth responds to youth, I'm afraid. Go over and tell the young chaps that they are here to socialize, not to stay together like stick-in-the-muds."

But, all my dictatorial skills disappear at a school dance. I didn't want to hand out orders to socialize. "Perhaps if we give them some more time, they'll warm up," I said.

But Mrs. Smith had waited long enough. Everything has its scheduled place in her scheme of the universe, and school dances are the place where there is dancing, *regardless of whether anyone wants to dance or not! Aside from her dedication to the order of her universe, Mrs. Smith was anxious to have action to observe and was disappointed at my reluctance to start some. I began to perceive my role more clearly— I was the catalytic agent that had to act before everything solidified into a frozen state.*

Mrs. Smith worked out a strategy to get the boys to dance —a game. Two hats were passed around, one for the boys and one for the girls, and everyone picked a number. Then the matching numbers formed a dancing couple. This was an emergency move, a last resort, and when the music stopped

Mrs. Smith called for everyone to swap partners with the nearest couple (private schools prepare you for all sorts of things).

At last the dancing was gaining a momentum of its own, but it was still too shaky for Mrs. Smith to relax. As soon as the last record was over she rushed to flip over the pile before anything but the music came to a halt. Dancing resumed, and now Mrs. Smith was able to observe things— who was dancing, and who wasn't, who couldn't, and who wanted to but wasn't asked. Who asked the boys and who just stood shyly in the corner sabotaging her evening of fun.

The best looking boy now came up to Mrs. Smith and surprised her by asking her to dance. "Thank you, my dear, but I wouldn't think of depriving one of the girls of the opportunity to dance with an attractive young man." Attractive young man then walked right past the girls and joined his group, who were giggling.

When the dance had ended, the boys shook hands with Mrs. Smith and thanked her for God knows what. Even the girls seemed relieved that the evening was over. Mrs. Smith and I stood in front of the school waiting for the girls to get into taxis.

"Imagine, Miss Frankfort, early in the year it was seriously suggested that these dances be abolished because the boys and girls did not enjoy themselves. I think you can see for yourself how silly a suggestion that is." Indeed, I could. Somewhere the evenings brought back a glimpse of youth which Mrs. Smith would not sacrifice. As I insisted that she take the next taxi, and even helped her in, she winked once more and for the first time all evening, looked a bit tired.

Mrs. Smith went off to attend her invalid husband. The girls and I remained waiting for taxis under the protective glare of the school caretaker, who was waiting for us to disappear so he could turn off the entrance lights and return to sleep in his basement quarters. And in those few minutes I discovered my real calling at Andrews—which was not to coerce boys into dancing with girls, but to form social consciences in my developing young ladies who were so ripe for idealism and for larger notions of morality than the ones Mrs. Smith considered. They were bored with the dance, bored with the boys, and very concerned that one of the Andrews black students would not be able to find a cab to take her home to Harlem. Spontaneously, as we all stood waiting, we started to talk about prejudice. Several of the sleepyheads woke up and became serious. We all agreed to continue the discussion and others on Wednesday afternoons after class.

I'll continue this letter some afternoon after class.

———◆◀◉▶◆———

"Who is going to take notes, Miss Frankfort? I mean minutes. Can I be secretary?"

"Girls, I must warn you. Parliamentary procedure brings out the dictator in me. Why don't we try it without minutes and see how it goes. Don't look so shocked, La Verne, I'm not suggesting we try it without clothes."

"But how will you remember what happens?"

"Don't you remember what's important to you? When are you ever going to learn spontaneity?"

"Why don't you tell that to Mrs. Smith?"

"Because Mrs. Smith has her own ways of doing things, and I am not trying to proselytize."

"To what?"

"Convert someone else to my way of thinking."

"Oh, that's not true, Miss Frankfort, you try to convert us to your way of thinking all the time."

"Do I?"

"Yes," the whole group shouted.

"Well, basically I'm a benevolent dictator, but only with people who are inferior to me in rank—like students. With my peers, I'm democratic."

"I don't follow you," Barbara said.

"Miss Frankfort just doesn't like phoniness. Right, Miss Frankfort?"

"If the slums are so bad, Miss Frankfort, why don't the people move?"

"Miss Frankfort, I have to leave now," La Verne whispered. "I forgot that Wednesday afternoons are not a good time for me because I have my singing lessons. I don't think I'll be able to come anymore."

"She didn't really have to leave so early. Her lessons aren't until much later. La Verne just thinks she's above social issues, you know, like all the black bourgeoisie," Miriam said.

The other Negro in the group, Alma Mae, remained silent throughout.

"Anyway, whenever you go through Harlem, how come you see these new cars and TVs if these people are so poor?" Barbara asked.

"First of all, there aren't really that many new cars. It's

just that people like us tend to notice anything shiny and new in a slum because it stands out so."

"And besides, a lot of those things are bought on time and taken away," Miriam added.

"How do you know?"

"Barbara, you take a look at a used car section in a newspaper and see the number of cars that are being sold because they were not paid up."

"What happens to the money they've already paid?"

"That's it. Gone."

"But that's not fair," Barbara said.

"Well, it's just a very expensive rental system for poor people."

"How come there are so many wrecked cars in Harlem?"

"Why do you think?"

Miriam spoke up. "Harlem is the junkyard for everything. Wrecked cars, wrecked bottles. . . ."

"And wrecked people," Alma added softly.

"And also, Miss Frankfort, people think the poor shouldn't have any luxuries like TV."

"Well, they shouldn't if they don't have money," Barbara said. "A luxury is something you buy when you have everything you need."

"How would you know, Barbara? You've always had everything you need and all the luxuries too, so you can't talk."

"If *you* just had nothing but basic needs all the time, not even one little luxury, life would be pretty grim, don't you think?" Miriam asked.

"Oh, I don't know," Jane said. "When we lived in Vermont we didn't have too many luxuries, as you call them, but I think we were very happy. We knew how to enjoy the simple things in life which the people in the city really don't know about."

"Like what, Jane?"

"Oh, like about animals, for instance."

"That's not so. We have two poodles at home."

"And we've had a hamster and a canary and a cat in our apartment."

"But still you don't see them in their natural setting."

"We do in our country house. We even have horses and cows. Any animal you can think of I've seen."

"Well, you may have *seen* them, Barbara, but did you milk the cows and watch them grow?"

"Oh, sure."

"Okay, but did you walk every day a long ways to school through fields?"

"I don't have to," Barbara answered. "I can see all the trees I want in Central Park from my bedroom window, and what's more, we even grow trees on our penthouse."

"But still it's not the same as real nature," Jane said.

"Girls, no one is saying the country is better than the city or vice versa. Why do you think you have homes in the country if the city has all to offer that the country does?"

"Excuse me, Miss Frankfort, but you're wrong. I agree the country is different, but I also think it's better."

"I agree with Jane," Miriam said. "I think the city brings about bad things."

"Like what, Miriam?"

"Oh, everyone's a stranger to everyone else. Nobody is friendly."

"Is it different in the country?"

"Well, not where we live, because we don't know any of the people nearby. We just have weekend guests and they're all from the city. Oh, but in Vermont, it was different, Barbara. Everyone knew everyone else where I lived and everyone was friendly and nice."

"Then how come you moved?"

"I think that's a personal question, Barbara, and one you shouldn't ask. I never said it was heaven," Jane answered in a controlled and precise way.

"Miss Frankfort, could we make a trip to Harlem next week during our discussion time?"

"Okay, next week we'll go out into the field, as the anthropologists say."

"The who?"

"A-n-t-h-r-o-p-o-l-o-g-i-s-t-s. You should be able to figure that one out from our vocabulary work."

"But what does it really mean?" Barbara asked.

Alma Mae was waiting when the discussion group split up.

"Miss Frankfort, I don't know how to say this," she said, her eyes looking at the floor, "but I felt bad about something you said."

"What is that, Alma?"

She hesitated, for a long time. "Well, I guess it's just that I would prefer not to go next week."

"Why? You live in Harlem. You could be our guide."

"I know you don't really think this way, Miss Frankfort, but you talk as if we were another primitive tribe, and we really aren't. It's just that where we live is not as pretty as where most of the other girls live."

"Don't you think it's a good idea for the other girls to become conscious that there are great inequalities and differences in the way people in the city live?"

"Yes, that's good, but I don't think the people of Harlem should be studied. We're not specimens."

"Alma Mae, you're right, we won't go, but I'd like you to discuss what you've just told me with the rest of the group. I think it would be very helpful, just as it has been for me."

"Thanks," she smiled.

The very next day echoes of our discussion reverberated. Mrs. Smith approached me in her standard manner.

"Do you have a moment? I want to consult with you." Mrs. Smith was upset. "Why don't you come into my room."

I knew she must really be upset when she invited me into her room.

"The girls told me you ran a very interesting discussion yesterday afternoon. Now I think that is just fine, but since you have not been here too long, it is understandable that you are ignorant of why we avoid certain topics. You are not yet familiar with the backgrounds of the girls, and so it is perfectly natural for you to discuss things that are really rather sensitive. For instance, I think I should tell you for future reference that Alma Mae—a lovely girl, one of our best students, in fact—is the daughter of the Loeb family maid. And were it not for the Loebs, Alma would never be here. Alma is on complete scholarship, but the family would never even have *heard* of a school like Andrews if it were not for Mrs. Loeb; she has been giving clothes to Alma's mother throughout the years so Alma doesn't look out of place. And there *is* a father in the family. He has a very nice job as a cook for Bellevue, and the whole family is really as lovely as a family can be. But of course they live in a slum building, although it is immaculate inside. As clean as your house or mine, if not cleaner.

"I also heard that La Verne left. La Verne isn't interested in very much that doesn't center around La Verne. *I* can't even get her interested in the Civil War. Now if I were a member of *her* group, I would certainly want to learn how I won my freedom. But not La Verne. She's just a scatterbrain, interested in boys, boys, boys like all the other scatterbrains. Of course, it is a problem socially for her, since she really feels part of the group, yet of course she can't socialize freely unless we can manage to find a Negro boy for her. And that is not always easy. You saw at the dance, although they promised to send us two, not one showed up."

Thursday P.M.

Canelli:

With the Discussion Group an official informal Andrews institution (which I am being paid *to take charge of) Mrs. Smith is beginning to perceive me as a real competitor. My advisory position has given me power; I was no longer confined to a curriculum; I can now talk openly about values and morality without accounting to Mrs. Smith. More later.*

———◄►———

"Ladies and gentlemen, no, pardon me, Mr. McMann will be joining us later. Let us commence at once, so we too will have time to partake of some holiday spirits when Mrs. Robbins arrives. Yes, Mrs. Smith, what is it?"

"Why don't we get the unpleasant business out of the way?"

"I second that, Agatha," said Miss Finch. "Surely we would not wish to be overheard discussing unpleasant matters when the head of our parents' association arrives. Especially since she'll be bringing us good tidings. And as we all know, they will be in a different form this year."

"Miss Millet, really, you need not take minutes today. This is merely an informal meeting before our Christmas farewell. What you might do, if you do not wish to sit idly by, is go downstairs and see how Maureen, Theresa, and Mary are managing with the eggnog."

"I'll go do that at once, but where shall I direct them to place the eggnog when we are ready to have it brought up?"

"Direct them to the center of my desk."

"Oh, Miss Langley, are you positive about that?"

"Absolutely. Can there be any doubts that my desk can withstand the weight of a bowl of eggnog?"

"But I was concerned with your papers and things."

"Let us not be concerned with anything but legitimate concerns."

"Which, Agatha, brings us right back to our unpleasant business."

"Go ahead, Florence, I haven't forgotten, but let us make it brief."

"I'll be as brief as I can be. Clearly Cassandra has violated our long-established democratic tradition of students not giving individual gifts to teachers, especially very wealthy students."

"How do we know it's Cassandra's doing and not her father's?"

"It's not the father, because the father is no longer living in the Fifth Avenue home, which is where the gift came from, nor, for that matter, is it that mother—I mean stepmother—who is off in Switzerland."

"Maybe the servants all ganged up and decided to give you a gift."

"Sybil, this is not the occasion for humor."

"Florence, may I say something? This does seem the perfect occasion for charity. Why can't you accept the gift if everyone is off somewhere and leave it at that?"

"Beatrice, you really do surprise me. Are you suggesting I accept a piece of jewelry—expensive, no doubt—from a girl who is on the verge of failing my class?"

"Now, Florence, let us hear a straightforward account of how the pin came to be presented. You say the gift was on your desk when you came back and Cassandra had already left."

"No. The chauffeur came up to my room, in person, and of course I saw no need to insult him by refusing the gift when he was only performing his duty."

"Then the family must be contacted. I see no other solution."

"What family, with the stepmother in Switzerland, the father God knows where, and only the servants left in the townhouse?"

"What about Cassandra herself?"

"*Cassandra* wasn't even sure where she was going. She thought she might be flying to Switzerland this afternoon, and even arrived with her luggage this morning. Of course after all the time Cassandra has been on her own, so to speak, you'd think she'd be bright enough to know what to do and what not to do."

"If she were bright enough to know better, Florence, she would not be flunking out of Andrews. I think the only thing we can do at this point is accept the gifts—that is, you, Florence, keep the pin and flunk Cassandra if she shows no improvement when she returns from Switzerland."

"If Cassandra flunks out, her father will surely withdraw the very generous offer he made to the school. Do you think it wise to insult the father without further thought?"

"Katherine, I have no more intention of insulting the father than of compromising the standards of Andrews. Until now we have managed without the gifts of Cassandra's family, and if need be, we can carry on without them in the future. All I am suggesting we do at the present time is have Mrs. Smith accept the gift, since I see no way of returning it without disturbing the servants again."

"You are right, Agatha. It does seem silly to disturb the household—whatever there is of it. But to wear the pin, of course, even if it *does* contain a real diamond I shall not do.

"I'm so happy we've worked out a compromise. It really enhances the spirit of brotherhood and forgiveness which I'm sure we all feel."

"Beatrice, we shall feel it a whole lot more if we bring forth the eggnog. Miss Millett, can you go down to see if it's ready and invite Mrs. Robbins into the room? I'm quite sure it was she who arrived while we were talking a few minutes ago."

"Is that you, John, poking your head inside? Your timing is almost perfect; the eggnog is on its way up."

"What makes you so sure I didn't come to see you, Sybil?"

"Because men don't. Not even my husband comes to see me."

"You British are very queer indeed."

"But, duckie, we do have mutual territory that we share."

"What is that, besides this bench?"

"Bench, my eye. It's a love seat, John. And won't you know it when the eggnog arrives."

"Not unless it's different this year from every other. I keep on telling them to forget the red bow around the ladle and just get a plain bottle of Scotch. See what I mean? Here it comes now, all pretty in preparation for one dainty shot."

"*Shot* of eggnog? That's like trying to kill someone with a beebee gun."

"I bet Beatrice and Florence get stoned with one shot. Well, hello, Mrs. Robbins, may I pour you some eggnog?"

"John, dear, so good to see you. I'll have a few sips to be sociable. If you pour any more I'll never fit into my bathing suit. And the holiday season has not even started."

"What's she talking about Lee?" I asked.

"Most of the parents go south for Christmas."

"That's fine, John. Thank you, I'm not very good at speeches, so you'll have to bear with me when I speak, not just for myself but on behalf of all Andrews parents in wishing you—the faculty—the happiest of holidays. I have been asked to inform you that as parents we do sympathize with the new spirit of practicality expressed to us through your wonderful headmistresses. And now speaking for myself as a mother with one daughter in the upper school, one daughter in the lower school and one daughter about to enter the nursery. . . ."

"How's the eggnog coming along?" said Sybil.

"It's going, not coming," quipped John.

"Just like me. Can you pour another shot, old chap?"

"Imagine missing Mrs. Robbins' speech, all for the love of Sybil."

"Now don't go blaming it on me, John. Just down your eggnog and shut up. Tooley just turned around to stare at us."

"That's all right, here come the checks."

"I want to especially thank Miss Langley, who first brought it to the attention of the Andrews parents that the faculty was having an increasingly harder time budgeting and would appreciate a gift more in keeping with their needs. I hope that this more practical gesture of our gratitude will help all of you have a wonderful holiday, and now I must run and attend to my own family, and I'll see you all afterwards."

December 23

Merry Christmas, Canelli,

While the Hasidic are lighting Chanukah candles, kids at Andrews are trying on bathing suits to take on cruises to the Caribbean while I march through "Julius Caesar" before the vacation starts. One poor child is flying to Switzerland because nobody but servants are in the many mansions her famous TV celebrity father owns, and who wants to spend Christmas alone with the servants in a mirrored mansion on Fifth Avenue?

Peace on the earth, good will toward women. I am now a hundred dollars richer than I was before the meeting, so I mustn't be too uncharitable in describing it. This is the year we down traditions and hail innovations—and hence, at Andrews, the first time that the teachers are being given money instead of the usual designer dresses presented straight from the daddies' showrooms. Poor Mrs. Smith was really torn. Designer dresses were an old Andrews tradition.

Even Tooley admitted that a gift is not really a gift when it isn't all wrapped up in a box, and Finch shuddered at the mention of cash value, while simultaneously worrying about hurting the feelings of the parents, although designer dresses have never been quite her cup of tea. Nevertheless she did think it might be more "in keeping with the spirit of Christmas" to go on accepting what the parents have always given rather than trying to change things and hurting their feelings. Langley assured her the parents were made of tougher stuff than their dresses and offered to assume all responsibility for insult should the faculty decide to ask for money (shudder, shudder), in lieu of dresses.

However, when a vote was taken at the last official faculty conference, I witnessed the first unanimous decision—cash! If Andrews was founded by wealthy German Jews who made their money in banking and finance, why should the present faculty have to accept the rags that the current Andrews parents have converted into riches? True, cash is not quite in keeping with the New England tradition, but are designer dresses any more so? I gather my gift was the measliest since I am so "junior" a member, and that middling Mrs. Smith received three hundred dollars, while the top of the hierarchy —Miss Langley and Tooley, got five hundred a head, which they then handed over to the scholarship fund, hopefully not out of some misguided guilt. When they invited anyone else who felt so inclined to do likewise, no one felt so inclined, not even Finch.

John McMann, who has already been the recipient of Andrews largesse in the form of his wife, started helping himself to a happy holiday as he and Sybil Bollinger picked up the eggnog ladle all wrapped up with a big red ribbon like the one around Miss Tooley's neck. The Schrafft's ladies came around with cookies the parents' maids had made before the parents took off on the Grace Lines for Curaçao or someplace sunny. On the mantle over the fireplace, which was lit, were Christmas cards carrying news of births and marriages (sequence uncertain) of previous Andrews alumnae.

We each took a rounded silver cup, offspring of the silver punch bowl, gifts of the class of '25, and then Miss Langley asked the Schrafft's ladies to please help themselves to a cup of eggnog. When the ladies stopped giggling and thanking her profusely, Miss Langley handed them each a card containing money we had all contributed. All blushed with the same embarrassed appreciation, the kind that comes from receiving when it is your habit to give.

There was sufficient eggnog for two drinks each and then some, which Mr. McMann insisted on finishing since he so hates to see waste. We all wished one another a happy vacation; Mrs. Smith pointed out that vacations were not really vacations for those devoted to the art of teaching, while old Langley said she thought a vacation should be precisely that. She for one did not intend to take home a stitch of work, but of course could not be sure that her partner would behave in so sensible a fashion and already suspected that Katherine would not. The likelihood is she'll sneak into the study one night and work, Langley predicted. Miss Tooley publicly promised to do no such thing, at least not until after the Christmas presents were laid out and the tree had been decorated from top to bottom.

I don't know when it happened, but at some point I started to get depressed about Christmas at Andrews. Maybe because it starts out too early, and there's none of that feeling of rush the way it is with the public schools when only one day is left to go shopping, get a tree, wrap the gifts. Do you remember those Christmas parties our teachers were always threatening not to have but which we knew they couldn't resist even if a major riot broke out? And how we would all wrap up the junky toilet water, the flowery handkerchiefs, and the boxes of stationery in Christmas paper and red and green bows, and what an honor it was to help carry the shopping bags loaded with our cheap presents down to their cars, while the teachers held onto the plants they were taking home for the week, afraid they would not survive the five days unattended? Do they still have those parties where teachers hand out little napkins edged in holly and all tied with ribbons and holding together the packet of penny candies—jelly beans, tootsie rolls, and the one peppermint stick, in its own cellophane wrapping, protruding from the packet like the top of an iceberg. And do teachers still leave twenty minutes to clean up messes which are never made in order to avoid returning to an imagined dirty room at the start of a clean year? And do the kids still think it clever to say, "See you next year" when next year is a few days away?

If none of this still goes on, please do not let me know. I like to remember those classroom parties—the highlights of the public school season held right before the week of church and a little loneliness. No one at Andrews worries about leaving a plant alone in a dark building, and students here equate vacations with cruise wear and don't make a big spiel over anything but the proper fit of a bathing suit. The faculty, too, views Christmas differently; there are visits from family and old friends, college chums passing through town, country homes with fireplaces where former roommates "winter"; it's a time to drop a line to let old acquaintances know how busy you are just keeping up with the usual, and with college class notes and alumni bulletins to be gone over.

There is church going too, either in small New England churches that are used for town meetings or the old established one on Fifth and Madison Avenues where oratories are sung more professionally than on recordings. Langley goes up to the family farm in Connecticut with her two sisters to celebrate Christmas in a simple way after Kate leaves for the Midwest to visit her retired colonel father. But both stay in the city Christmas Eve and decorate a tree which I am sure Langley gnawed down herself. The younger teachers with families in other parts of the country go home for the holiday weekend and then return to attend theatre, ballet, and Christmas concerts but not museums and stores, which are mobbed with kids. Lee will go ice skating during the week, and Sybil just wants a brisk walk through the park to clear the American air out of her lungs. Hope will not return to Iowa until she sees the Fifth Avenue store windows and catches B. Altman's puppet show, although she knows the one at Lord & Taylor is even better, but the lines there are too long.

I shall probably go crazy, trying to bring forth memories of stingy characters who can't spare a penny, whom I never knew except through books. I confess, I miss a sense of deprivation. It's hard to appreciate largesse without some suffering. I even resent the Salvation Army Band for looking too prosperous, mainly because it's not cold enough for their noses to run and get red at the tips. I ask you, how can you have Christmas without those little Irish churchmice teachers who believed in all the fake tinsel straight from the Five and Ten? I don't want elegant sterling silver eggnog bowls purchased by some grateful alumnae who've been basking in the Bahamas.

How am I going to whip up some holiday spirit, Canelli?

January 7

Well, on to the new year. Have you ever read hospital records reporting the progress of some dread disease which can be checked only if drastic measures are immediately taken? Or prison reports on a defective personality whose chances for rehabilitation rest solely on a willingness to take advantage of wholesome outside influences? Either case will do—if you want to understand the model for private school reports, which I am supposed to be writing. The general rule is to say something positive and something negative for each student in such a fashion as to reassure the parent that the child is learning something, but is by no means exhausting all the chal-

lenges Andrews offers. With the brightest girls there is no problem, you just think of some minor flaw. With the mediocre ones, you tell the truth—a little bit of good and a little bit of bad. It's the ones that are really floundering who make for difficulty in the world of diplomacy. Today at the first post-holiday faculty conference we were given guidelines for handling these cases.

"You might say, 'For a child of her potential, Susan is on her way to becoming an underachiever,'" Langley offered as a concrete example of tact.

"But what if the child does not have much potential to start with?" Mrs. Smith inquired. "Those are the ones who cause the greatest difficulty." (The "those" were usually sisters of Andrews alumnae or daughters of men with lots of money and political connections who sometimes produce the dumbest offspring as if by some law of decompensation.)

"In such a case," Langley answered, "you give the child some credit: 'Wendy tries hard but is not yet in control of the material, an indication that her efforts, while not entirely absent, are clearly not completely present.'"

By now I had grasped the basics—draw out a statement so that it rises like a thin piece of hair, all teased up to give the appearance of saying something. After the conference, some report cards from previous years were passed around for the benefit of the new faculty members (meaning myself). Here is one by a former English teacher:

"A native facility with spoken words often leads Barbara into confusing circumlocution, which in turn reduces her ability to organize her thoughts in the most logical manner possible."

This is the standard politely worded threat that the child is on the verge of becoming an idiot, and when a more gentle but equally ominous note is to be sounded, you say that "the child's grades do not reflect his true potentialities"—which if allowed to remain untapped may turn into petrified wood.

From a history teacher: "Lois' ideas tend to be occasionally fragmentary, at times abstruse, but nevertheless promising by and large. Perhaps if her inhibition in penmanship were improved, her aversion to strict organization might cease to be."

After the grades and comments from individual teachers were completed, Tooley and Langley added a postscript—some overall comment on the child's general performance. Tooley was always cheery in tone. "Well, Vicki, after all is said and done, this report reflects a good term for you. I look forward to continued improvement from you in the spring." "Keep at it," was a favorite Tooleyism, in keeping with Kansas corn and pioneer spirit. Negative things were always spoken of as "bad tendencies." Average records were described as "respectable, although below top college standards," and nondescript students always wound up as "pleasures to have in the classroom"—like the nonworking fireplaces.

It's a beautiful challenge to write these reports—after spending a semester talking about the need for clarity and simplicity in writing, and being direct, true to impressions, and economical with words—and why good writing omits modifiers, qualifiers, and adjectives.

Speaking of adjectives, Miriam is this bright intense girl whose Greek shoulder bag fell over in assembly. And what should come spilling out and rolling down the aisle one morning right in the middle of the school song but her diaphragm.

And who spied the rubber shape on its way down? Mrs. Smith, who did nothing until the school song was over and the diaphragm was at rest. Then she took a Kleenex from her bag, lifted the diaphragm off the floor just like she was picking up a dead mouse, and walked to the back of the hall with the thing wrapped in Kleenex which she covered with her bag. I'm not sure what she did with it after that. She did *confide to me later that it was the first time she had to* touch *one of those things, and she is the mother of. . . .*

Miriam is now at Hillside Hospital.

Tuesday

At Andrews it all starts at age 3, and for the most foolish and least independent, school ties never end. But I still do admire the quality of the education, which is the one reason why I think I should stay on. Even at a second-rate private school, the girls receive a superior education compared to the one you get in public schools. Everything possible is done to make a child learn—small classes, individual instruction, guidance, and endless encouragement. At Andrews the stability and discipline are so much a part of the overall structure that people like me don't have to worry about discipline problems. When a place is supplied with a strong head, the teachers are freed of the need to act in an authoritative manner. That's one of the ironies of traditional private schools—in some ways they're more informal. It's as if you can throw anything against a sturdy brick wall and not have to worry about its cracking.

Wednesday

Langley's whole way of accepting things and Carrying On

.126.

No Matter What is something I'm trying hard to copy. You would call it coping, and maybe that is what it amounts to. I think I told you in one letter about Sybil Bollinger, a British teacher with impeccable credentials who turns out to be the only faculty member not invited back. Simply couldn't cope with things, and all the perfect pronunciation in the world couldn't cover that up. Langley once said, "Something is happening to the English Empire." I love Langley's ability to connect up all sorts of phenomena and link them to the largest trends of civilization.

◀━━━◆▶━◆▶

The class valedictorian was going to Vassar. Naturally. Anything else would have been a personal insult to at least Miss Tooley. The valedictorian accepted Vassar but the second highest rejected Vassar for Smith. The bright but poor scholarship Negro was going to Barnard, where she'd be able to get a good education while she continued to live at home and help raise her younger brothers and sister. The rich Negro student was going to Finch, like several of the girls who were not really academic but who did well in Mr. McMann's college level course in art history. The one who wrote the best thesis in art was going to Sarah Lawrence. And the girl who did exceptionally well in science was going to Mount Holyoke.

Miss Tooley was busy making a million calls, since it was her responsibility to see that everyone goes somewhere. Not getting a girl into a college was like leaving her free to wander the streets in sin. But of course, what else are private schools for if not to give rich kids an edge in college admissions? Andrews would fold up faster than a little shop if Tooley couldn't produce a good college admissions record. Tooley was no magician. She could only work with what material she'd been given, pushing it along, selecting the best channels, detouring when necessary, dropping this course or that, but never inflating the marks too much because "what will happen next year when we apply if we overrate the girls this year."

As for the rejections, she dried her eyes and took to the telephone. Tooley was much less inhibited about happiness than about tragedy. Rejections were no crying matter; they called for action. "We will find something. No girl of mine is going to leave here without a place to go," she announced at the special meeting for rejected seniors. "This is not a school which trains gypsies, and there are lots of little places. True, they may not be Vassar or Holyoke, no one here may have heard of them, but if you want an education you can get one anywhere. There are dozens of little colleges all over the Midwest, and some of them are right on lakes." She actually sounded happy at the thought of sending someone to a little college near a little lake where she said it might even be easier to get a good education.

Tooley may have overlooked the fact that the girls who were accepted nowhere did not want a good education. But Tooley lost sight of things when she tried to square the outside universe with her own. It's Langley who understood that girls who had lived in New York all their lives and had spent every Saturday shopping since they were old enough to spell Bonwit's were not going to be thrilled at the idea of a little college near a little lake in the Midwest.

Langley advised Tooley to advise the girls to go to the city colleges, or design school or fashion institutes not too far from good clothing and Wall Street where the good men are. Sound advice. Except we could do without the clothing, please.

I thought I had grown accustomed to ceremony. (Had I not been the star of a Hasidic celebration before even coming to Andrews?) But there is a difference between spontaneous, fanatic joy and formal, well-rehearsed ritual. The first sign that the Andrews graduation would be more like the latter was a request for the size of my robe and the colors of my alma mater for the ribbons on the hood—as well as any additional information about additional degrees that form further draperies around your neck. There I was at the end of May with a robe and ribbons, marching at the very end (being the most junior faculty member) of a procession in a ceremony that vacillated between a state inauguration, an Oxford Convocation, and a Jewish wedding. The trouble with people who bury their own traditions is that they substitute a nothing-but-the-best way of thinking as if they are looking for a surgeon or a shoe and only the top quality will do. Here, the quality was always measured by money—how much something cost.

Langley, thank God, balanced the excesses with her own instinctive moderation. I knew that unless Langley died before graduation, the affair would not be hideous because Langley would not conduct a hideous affair, unless it was to raise money, which the graduation exercises clearly were not designed to do. From the start Miss Langley, introduced a note of solemnity to offset the relish with which Miss Tooley savored ceremony. I think she feared that someone would get up and read telegrams of congratulations as she headed the formal procession down the aisle of Town Hall where the graduation was held.

For an entire week before graduation, morning after morning was devoted to rehearsing. The girls were taught how to walk with their heads straight ahead, never looking at the relatives in the audience who would try to catch their eye. At times it was like being back at the Yeshiva. The girls could not be casual and serious and solemn, they were giggly and excited and anxious even during rehearsals.

"We're lucky the event is to be held in the evening," Mrs. Smith said to me at the last rehearsal. "Perhaps the girls will have less energy then," as if fatigue creates an air of solemnity. She herself was exhausted from her efforts to teach the girls how not to spoil things. It was as if four years of education would be wasted if the girls did not go through this ceremony correctly. And surely a lot of time *would* have been wasted if they did not perform correctly, for so much of private school life *is* an initiation into ceremonial behavior—luncheons, dinners, teas. Private schools are really little academies for learning protocol.

Mrs. Smith became maudlin the day before graduation, but got hold of herself the evening of the event—not a tear in her eye. She instructed us all to wear black dresses, for the on-stage effect would be ruined by color. "A plain black dress, preferably cool. It can get hotter than blazes up under the lights, and we do not want to wilt away before the evening is over. What's more, if you are the type who perspires," and here she stared hard at me, "do wear something sleeveless and of light material. For it is most unbecoming to have a formal group on stage wiping sweat from their faces. Please try to avoid that if possible. If you think there is a chance that you will perspire to the point where it is necessary to wipe your face, carry a dainty white handkerchief with you. There are pockets in the robes, and don't forget to install one there. In no event is anyone to wipe the sweat off one's face with anything but a handkerchief. And another crucial point. You must remember to bring the invitation; otherwise you will have to get hold of Miss Langley or Miss Tooley to gain entry to the hall, since the guards have been trained to be strict.

"I myself have seen old Andrews alumnae who quickly forget that the relatives of the present graduating class must be admitted before former students, no matter how faithful, for graduation is a very carefully planned affair. We know the exact number of seats, and we have printed our invitations in accordance with that information. So please do not interfere with this long planning by either forgetting your tickets or coming too late or some other silly thing."

Then came a word from Langley to the girls. "Please, no crying, before or during the ceremony. I shall not be touched by such tears."

"Now I would like to add a word, girls," said Miss Tooley. "I cry easily, so I can sympathize with those among you who may be tempted. But do as I do, save your tears for later. Once the ceremony is over, you can let go. Ceremonies are ruined by too early a display of emotion."

"By *any* display of emotion," Miss Langley corrected.

And why shouldn't the girls have been emotional after twelve years of practice in the rituals that become graced with time—the school songs, the school productions, the annual evening when the girls satirize the faculty, who have a year to steel themselves for the enjoyment of it. And now this, the ultimate ritual, graduation, "the end and the beginning," as Mrs. Smith said so many times that I could not believe that there *was* any ending.

And for most of the girls there was no ending; they retained close ties to the school by making class reunions and get-to-gethers a regular part of their "calendar." By the time they graduated they had learned lesson number one: young ladies have calendars, and life is spaced according to events, which, like the seasons, have a life of their own.

After all the warnings and rehearsals, it seemed inevitable that something should go wrong. I arrived early in a light sleeveless dress plus a dainty white handkerchief, since I not only suspected I would sweat but *knew* I would, even if it were zero on stage. I was nervous. It was the first time I had been part of a procession as something other than a student. Town Hall was softly lit; the red carpeting was regal in an inconspicuous way and the chandeliers with their soft lighting were soothing to my nerves. I might have been attending a chamber music concert if I did not have to go backstage to the dressing room where the faculty was putting on robes. I stepped into my gown and eased into my role of rear guard of the procession—which meant I was the last person to march. And since the faculty was an uneven number, I marched down alone, in the middle of the aisle, neither too far to the right nor too far to the left, gauging myself by Lee and Sybil, who were marching before me.

Sybil kept changing steps to get in time with the music and looking all about for familiar faces. She even turned around to me and said, "How you doing, chum?" As I stared straight ahead I could see the procession, led nobly by Miss Langley, erect and tall, making the line a bit asymmetric. I could not see Miss Tooley until the procession turned to head up the stairs onto the stage. Miss Tooley looked red; I prayed that she would not have a heart attack and that I would not start sweating too soon.

The whole thing was impressive, formal, and filled with appropriate pomp, and yet I felt more like a flower girl at a wedding. I could hear parents oohing and ahing, and even some sniffling. I could sense the anticipation of the graduates waiting behind me, ready to march as soon as the faculty was all on stage. But not once did I look behind, remembering Orpheus and Euridice and other things that had nothing to do with the goings on. Once on stage, I regained a sense of what it was all about, and along with the other faculty members observed "our" girls march down the aisle with their white robes, virginal and pretty, carrying bouquets and just about managing to conceal their glee about the end and beginning of their Andrews days. Except for the dim lights in the hall and the red carpeting and the fancy attire of the parents, whom I could barely perceive, the girls reminded me very much of "my" Yeshiva children. I hoped they were as happy.

At the farewell faculty meeting the following day everyone agreed that the graduation had gone well. "The amount of hysteria did not exceed the normal," Mrs. Smith stated as if reporting on a laboratory specimen. The hysteria was limited to the parents, who kissed their daughters and some of the teachers. Even Miss Tooley waited until she was no longer under stage lights before her eyes flooded with tears. Miss Langley shook her valedictorian with two hands rather than using her customary one-handed shake. But she never held on too long, as if a hearty double handshake could lead to something more emotional. For if she let go, who would be there to stem the tide, hold up the dike, and do all the other things that keep emotions in their place. Mrs. Smith's eyes merely got watery, as if she had a speck of dust in them. But if you looked at her hands you could see them trembling.

I noticed that at the last meeting of the school year. I think the end of the school year frightened Mrs. Smith the way nighttime frightens children—the darkness of days without discipline problems, crises, major and minor, communications, secret and open. I decided Mrs. Smith was very human, and I no longer condemned her.

Finally everyone said good bye mainly because they had to "get down to the business of summering."

Part of the beauty of a private school is that there are people to worry about getting you into college and you are taken care of. People are paid to worry for you; it is part of their job. When the school semester is over, private school kids can go on a guided teen tour to Europe and even *want* to get some more culture because private education is not contaminated with competition. Once you are in the private schools you are assured that someone feels a moral commitment to see you through to somewhere, because no private school wants its alumni just hanging about. It's poor advertising, and private schools must worry about money all the time. If you get into a good private school, someone will see to it that you are not left stranded. A Miss Tooley will make her last minute long distance telephone call to someplace and plead politely and with dignity that you are a decent person who with the right kind of atmosphere, not too much pressure, can do well; that you are, though admittedly not a brilliant student, nevertheless one whom it is a pleasure to know, for you are a lady and what's more a thoroughly nice person, which should count for something.

I had survived my first year at Andrews, but only because I'd been able to pour out my feelings to Canelli: The question now was would *I* cope with the summer and the long hours? I sat thinking of summer as a time when nametags were sewn onto shorts, socks, and other camp paraphernalia; school was over for a while, and if you were lucky this year you would really learn how to swim. But mainly summer was heat and boredom and sitting on stoops waiting for the Good Humor man to come around with his special of the week and deciding whether it was worth risking something like huckleberry ice cream. For me, it was watching the boys play baseball in the school yard every day until the sun got too hot and then, when they left, sitting and talking with other kids who lived on the block, and who begged for five minutes more to stay out when their mothers shouted for them to come home. Summer was having projects like learning how to knit or counting a hundred cream-colored convertibles and then waiting for the first boy who spoke to you—who would be your husband.

·❧FOREST❧··

Labor Day

Dear Canelli,

    Brace yourself for news. It's all over, but I'm still not jobless. I didn't even have to beg Andrews to take me back after having told them I was leaving. I couldn't see myself returning to that silly, charming world and carrying on like a brave pioneer in a wood-paneled frontier. I needed a new connection to the world, and I have found one.

Forest is a small progressive private school in the heart of the city, or (to be more exact, geographically speaking) the groin. But first a detour.

Two years ago I wrote to one Nellie Coomstock, a lady who runs a little school half a block way from where I live, to inquire about a job. When I received no answer, I resigned myself to the fact that the only way you can teach in a good private school is by being an alumna or a relative, or by happening along just at the time of a teacher's breakdown, as at Andrews. Evidently everyone at Forest was in good shape when I wrote for a job; it was only last week that I received a call from Nellie Coomstock answering my letter from two years back.

No, she had not forgotten me. How could she, with that charming handwritten note? It's not often she gets such an informal-looking job request. Could it be she was equating my unprofessional letter with individuality, nonconformity, community, craft, and probably even flowers and trees? The fact that I was too lazy to type out a formal résumé did not occur to Nellie Coomstock, who put my handwritten note away for some needy future day. And so the morning after that needy day, I headed down the block toward Forest armed with my big teacher pocketbook. The pouch still contained some chalk from my Yeshiva days, undoubtedly a gift from you to me.

Picture a group of boys and girls with long straight hair who looked as if they have just stepped out of a bittersweet folk ballad, but who had in fact just locked up their bicycles and who were now standing in front of the entrance waiting for the caretaker to open up the school. Add some parents dressed in ponchos and serapes of rough, intensely colored cloth like those worn by Peruvian peasants. And at least one such parent carrying in a backsling a babe who hasn't quite come of age to start classes—which in the private school world means about six months. Now keep in mind the location, half a block from my home, and you should understand why I've been longing to teach at Forest. It's a school where the kids can't wait to get inside, even on the sunniest days, and if kids feel that way, I figured the place must be heaven for teachers. Right?

I entered Forest, which is divided into two parts—Forest South, a set of three brownstones on one block, and Forest North, a parallel set on the next block, connected by a yard. I entered Forest South, the part I pass each day, and wham—colors assaulted me from all over, wiping out all memories of Andrews and its clubby cozy formality. The shock of contrast plunged me back to my own drab public school corridors.

At Forest, primary colors leap forth from the walls amid an atmosphere of bright chaos. I saw children in work pants all over the place, as I looked around for Nellie Coomstock or her office, if she had one. She saw me first and called out. "Come in as soon as you're ready. That is, look around as much as you'd like." And good voyeur that I am, I took an extra minute to look some more before entering the office, a small room filled with half-finished objects of every conceivable craft material. I helped myself to a seat on a wooden bench which Nellie said was made by Warren the Wobbly Cobbler, as the children call him.

"They've even written a poem. It's hanging right above

you." I looked up and sure enough there was a poem, beautifully lettered. Next to the poem was a picture of Warren at
work. I turned to look at Warren at work and almost slipped
off his wobbly bench.

"The best way you'll learn about us is by looking and listening—the best way anyone learns about anything—which of
course is what Forest is about," said Nellie.

Nellie is a big-boned girl of about 50, dressed in a plain tailored blouse and skirt and flat walking shoes. Her getup would
be indistinguishable from that of a meter maid or visiting nurse,
were it not for dark stockings tucked into her sensible shoes
and a twisted piece of copper hanging on a leather strap all
the more conspicuous against her starched white blouse. Nellie caught me staring at it and informed me it was "free-form
jewelry" made in one of the shops. On the table which served
as her desk there were ceramic pieces, some very lovely, others
less so. When I commented on them, she said, "Yes, we keep
them all, especially those rescued from moments of destructive
despair."

"What a nice contrast to most schools, where only the finished and the best are kept on display," I said.

"Knock, knock, Nellie, I'm coming in," a small child inter-
rupted. "I must speak to you."

"But I am speaking to someone, love."

"Well, it can't wait, Nellie, I mean it."

"Well, then, waste no time and tell me." A postman from
the eights, Billy, had been carrying a special delivery letter to
the tens and he lost it. "Well, what's the problem?" Nellie
asked. "You know what to do in such a case, Noah."

"Here's the problem. If we do it as they do it in the real post office, then the tens won't get the letter in time to attend the play of the nines, who decided to invite the tens at the last minute. But I think it's cheating if we make another letter and do the whole thing over from scratch, because no post office would do it that way, and I think if we're running a real post office we should do things the real way."

Nellie agreed with Noah "one hundred percent" and told him to just go right back and convince the others. "You see, that's how learning takes place here," she said proudly.

Shortly another child came in, this time without any "knock, knock." "Nellie, are we supposed to print up the library cards or the letterheads for the Parents Association this week?" Nellie was a little less patient this time and said "How am I supposed to know? Why don't you ask your foreman of the week what the schedule is, Michael?" But it turned out that Michael was the foreman of the week.

"Then surely you must know more about it than I. Go back and figure it out with your workers."

"But the head clerk from the store just sent in an emergency order for stationery, and I don't know what to do," said Michael, who seemed verged between tears and wetting his pants. When he settled on tears, Nellie said, "Whatever you do, don't cry, Michael, because that won't solve the problem. I think you and the chief clerk should have a meeting and get things in order in both his shop and your workroom. Obviously someone has been negligent in the record keeping, and it is your responsibility to find out who."

"Shit," said Michael and walked out.

Now Nellie looked at me. When I disappointed her by not wincing, she went into a little speech anyway. "We don't fuss much about foul language here. If things get too extreme and an epidemic of bathroom talk breaks out, I have a very simple solution. I go up and repeat for half an hour every foul word I know, and when the class is sufficiently bored, I leave. It's never failed to cure the plague." Why, oh why, Canelli, do private schools always think they are carrying on in the face of crises that don't exist?

Nellie now hit upon a real problem. "The most effective way to treat so-called problems is to ignore them, except for our one major problem—parents. We just can't make them disappear, although sometimes I sure wish we could. Forest does not believe—that is, the teachers here don't believe—that children cause problems when left on their own. We do believe what a child with a so-called problem is trying to tell us is that he has a problem parent—which of course most children do. . . .

"But look, Ellen, I've done enough talking. Why don't you explore us a bit and see what you think? Learn about us the way our children learn about the world—by looking around —which is a crucial part of our teaching philosophy. Of course, we don't have any formal philosophy here, because that too goes against our philosophy. So just wander about. You might like to visit a workshop this afternoon or play-acting this morning. It's entirely up to you. Nobody will object to your presence; chances are that they won't even notice it, because everyone is so absorbed in activity and also because we get so many visitors all the time. Many people come away

shocked, and you may yourself. In which event, you wouldn't want to be here.

"*Either a person fits or they don't,*" Nellie said looking directly at me. "*There is little room for middle-of-the-roaders here, and frankly we don't* mind *that we're considered shocking. We'd much prefer to be controversial than bland. As a matter of fact, the only children we consider problems are those* without *any. Why don't you spend the next day or two just looking, and if you like what you see you can come and teach.*"

Before turning me loose to learn on my own, Nellie gave me a few brief guidelines about what to look for. "You might start out with Yard and observe the children there, since Yard is our core outdoor activity. And then, let me see, why don't you take a peek at Play City, which the sixes run. Perhaps they'll invite you to a production this afternoon. Providing they like you, of course."

"*Who are the sixes, Nellie?*" I asked in order to get oriented.

"*Oh, we don't bother with fancy names the way other private schools do. Why call a grade a* form *or some other high-faluting term when you can call a group by its actual age? The sixes are the 6-year-olds, and we have threes through thirteens. Isn't that a lot simpler a way of doing things?*" And I agreed it was. "*One last piece of information. Each group, starting with the sixes, who are the first to attend school for a whole day, have a job to perform, since work is the core of our curriculum. It's an adult misconception that children find* pure *play fun. Children enjoy play only when it has a meaningful goal, where a* product *of some sort results. But here I* go talking again, and I said I wouldn't. It really goes against all I believe. That is, lecturing a newcomer is not the way to get to know us. Go out and explore on your own, and then we'll talk some more."

I set out from her office for the wilds of the exoticly colored hall, making my way toward Yard, not "the," but plain old Yard, the way Andrews was never anything but Andrews.

Canelli, have you figured out what private schools have against articles? Do you think "the" is plebeian? I mean, why does the omission of an article give a word a mystical meaning?

I made my way through the ground floor of the brownstone and came upon a back door. To Yard and Forest North, said a sign. I opened the door and there it was—Yard, a postage-sized piece of land surrounded on the south and north by the backs of brownstones dwarfed by the immense city buildings hovering over Forest. Nowhere was there a tree, but nature was not completely out of the picture. Peeking down through all the concrete was a snatch of sky above about the same size as the yard below.

If you didn't look sideways or upward and concentrated only on Yard, there were interesting things to see—first painted wood forms, mainly geometric, which the children were using to construct things. One group had taken three huge cubes and piled them on top of each other, and then rested a rectangular-shaped board at an angle to the cubes: A slide! Another had constructed an odd-looking sled from a board, and kids were taking turns pushing each other around. Here the fun seemed to be in having no handles, *which made a turn very tricky. But no one seemed to mind falling. If only the Yeshiva children could have rolled about these forms a bit. There is something so attractive about children leaping freely, jumping, and doing cartwheels on the ground. I've never seen such a physically fearless group. Several kids were climbing the fire escapes as if the brownstones were jungle gyms. None of them seemed at all self-conscious.*

Finally I lost my own self-consciousness and spoke to a child. (Here's me trying to be free without first climbing a fire escape:) "Hi, there. I'm a visitor. Can you tell me what this activity Yard is all about?"

"Sure, it's like this," said one boy. "You see, we live in an urban industrial society that stinks."

I looked up at the smoke pouring out of the tall buildings above.

"Well, it's bad for the personality, I mean it makes you neurotic, which of course we all are anyhow. But that's beside the point. You know, our society doesn't care about play, just success."

"That's why we spend a lot of time in Yard," another child chimed in.

"What's your name?" I asked.

"Adam. What's yours?"

"Ellen." The spontaneity was contagious.

"Of course, the whole thing is a bit phony," said Adam, "but it's the only thing we can do in the city. When the school first started, the kids used to spend half the time in the country and half in the city. But that just doesn't work out anymore."

"So we just sort of spend time in Yard to be out in the fresh air."

Who was I to argue about the evils of urbanization or knock the rewards of the outdoors? But I didn't quite see how Yard provided a tie to nature. "Where is your Play City?" I asked.

"That's on the second floor of Forest North."

"Is it a room? I mean, how will I recognize it?"

"Don't worry," Eric assured me. "Everything here has a sign printed on it. The elevens run the printing presses, so everything is all printed up."

"What group is this out here?"

"We're the twelves."

"Thanks for all the information."

By now I was used to the colorful signs welcoming one, but Lord, I wasn't ready for a voice which squawked out "Forest North, Forest North" without stopping. Evidently the Nature Room had imprisoned a bird, who in turn took his revenge by screeching out all day long. He wasn't deluded; he knew what a real forest was. At this point I decided to leave for the day, in order to preserve my own dwindling supply of sanity.

More anon.

"Quick. Get me the hoses, Justin. We have no time to waste."

"Look, Dewey, here come the fireboats right down the river. Hurry, hurry, Justin."

"That's it, Nina, get the firemen on land to direct the hoses to the top of the warehouse." Dewey, a middle-aged lady, was jumping and gesticulating in all directions.

"What should we do with the food in the warehouse, Dewey?"

"Let's get the ladders up to the top before there's a collision with the fireboats and the barge. Someone please try to save the chickens."

"I bet they can see the flames in New Jersey."

"And even in Connecticut."

"You can't see from Connecticut, Billy. Can you, Dewey?"

"I don't know why anyone's worrying where you can see from while the fire's still burning."

"I mean Queens, anyway."

"You can't see it from Queens either, Billy."

"Boys, are you going to argue facts while the warehouse is in flames?"

"I think it's out now, Dewey."

Dewey stopped jumping up and down. "Good work, team," she said. "Now what was all the business about Connecticut and Queens?"

"Billy said you can see the fire from Connecticut, and Tommy said you couldn't," a little girl piped up.

"Billy is a silly billy, today. Come here and let's step into the center of the city."

Dewey pulled a little boy into a chalked-out area in the shape of an island, carefully avoiding the large paper skyscrapers that arose from the floor.

"Now, Billy, what's over there when we walk this way?" Dewey asked, pointing to her left.

"The Henry Hudson Parkway. I mean the West Side Drive."

"And what river runs along it?"

"The Hudson."

"What's on the other side of the Hudson?"

"New Jersey."

"Well, what has Connecticut got to do with New Jersey, Billy?"

"I don't know."

"Who can show me how to get to Connecticut from here? Come on, Duncan."

Another child stepped into the mapped-out area. "When we go to our house in Westport we drive over this way, then onto the East River Drive, and then we get to Connecticut a little later."

"When I go to our house we go past Macy's and Altman's and through the tunnel and we can see Connecticut."

"Then where is Jonathan's house? Who can tell?"

No one answered. "Jonathan, come up and drive to your house so everyone can follow your route." Jonathan got down on the floor and pretended to start up his car. "Wait, we have to stop to get gas."

"Johnny's got a tiger in his tank."

"Stop that foolishness, Tommy. I wish you would quit listening to those silly ads."

"Who has change for the tunnel?" Johnny said.

"Oh, I know, he's going to Brooklyn. When we go through a tunnel that's where we go."

"That's where *you* go, Carol, but is that where Johnny is going?"

"No," Johnny said. "We never go to Brooklyn. I'm going to Long Island. Long Island's where we keep our sailboat."

"How can that be if you're still in the tunnel?"

"I'm out of the tunnel now."

"No, you're not. You didn't pay the man yet."

"Okay," Johnny said, and handed a make-believe figure a make-believe coin. "Now we're at my house and there's our sailboat."

At the end of Johnny's trip, Dewey sketched in all the places on the chalk city.

"Dewey, when are we going on our garbage trip?"

"You mean when are we going to follow the garbage men on *their* trip? Who knows the next time the garbage men collect garbage? No one? Well, what's the way we find out when we don't know something? Look it up in an encyclopedia, did you say, Leon? Who knows a better way, a more reliable way to learn something?"

"We could watch and see when they come."

"Good. Who wants to keep track of the garbage men's schedule for the week so we can plan when to follow them? You, Steven? Fine."

"I thought we were going to follow the oil men next, Dewey."

"Well, there's nothing saying we can't do both. Let's first see the schedule of the garbage men and then decide. And now my little firefighters, it's time for fairy tales and some rest from fighting. Who wants to start with the first one?"

"I have one, Dewey, *The fire is swallowing the building*."

"Okay. That's a fine start, Timothy. Who'll go on with it?"

"*The building is thirsty. It will die unless some water comes quick.*"

"I don't like that, Dewey."

"Then start a tale of your own, Tommy."

"The bridge bent over the head of the boat."

"Who wants to do something with that?"

Soon the sixes tired of making up tales, and Dewey sent them on to lunch. Then she came over to me for the first time. "Hello. I'm Dewey."

"And I'm Ellen," I said, extending my hand.

"No need for formalities. What do you think of us?"

"I found the whole thing interesting. Especially the fairy tales. It struck me that. . . ."

"Let me interrupt you to explain a few things that you might not know. We intentionally discourage the telling of real fairy tales. I know that everyone thinks they are stimulating to a child's imagination, but we believe they just suppress it actually. It's like all secondhand information. They keep the child out of the real world. You saw how the children carried on with the fire. *That* is what stimulates a child's imagination, not some little creatures with frilly dresses who wave wands in the air. Before a child can understand the world of fantasy he must get to feel at home with the real world which is all around him, and it's our job to show him how to look. By comparison to real life, fairy tales are bloodless affairs, wouldn't you agree?"

"I've never thought of it that way, but I think it's an interesting idea."

"No, dearie, it is not an *idea*. We've been watching the results of miseducation for years now, and our ways are based on what we've seen. Nothing here is done according to some arbitrary idea. Everything has a reason based on experience, which is exactly why we don't like fairy tales. A child doesn't need fairy tales, which are just conveniences anyway for adults who are scared to let a child be free."

"How do the parents react?"

"Terribly. That is, at first. With time they usually come to appreciate our methods. We had one mother who took her son to Paris right after her divorce. Of course she wasn't in any state of mind to find her way about. But fortunately the child had developed such a good sense of direction from spending a year in Play City that she didn't have to worry. And that's at 7, which is why we don't fuss much with facts; we're more concerned with making a child alive and curious to the world around him. If a child has that, it's impossible for him not to pick up some facts eventually."

"What would you suggest I observe next?"

"Well, if you insist on being systematic, go see the sevens —they run the store. But you'll have to get to school early in the morning to see the store in operation. That's when it's open."

Next morning I arrived at the store—a windowsill with a table behind it and shelves for paper, pencils, and other school supplies—just as it was opening for business at 9:00 o'clock. Already there was a short line waiting for orders. "First customer, please," said a little boy behind the sill.

"Here I am," a ponytailed girl answered. "The nines need twelve red pencils." I watched as the sales clerk took out a piece of scrap paper and tried to figure out the cost.

"Let me see; two for a penny," he said to himself. "How many did you ask for again?"

"Twelve, please, and I'm in a hurry."

The clerk looked flustered and got up to consult his assistant for the day, who quickly came through with the total. "That will be six cents."

"I only have a dime," the girl said, impatiently. "Do you have change?"

The boy looked in his cash register. "Sorry, you'll have to come back later for your change."

"Well, please put it down on the receipt how much the store owes me."

The clerk took out his pad, but he seemed to forget the order again. Now the little girl became patronizing, and spoke slowly. "It's twelve pencils, at two for a penny, which comes to six cents. I'm in a rush," she added, as she put her hand on her hip and watched him prepare the order. The boy pressed down with his pencil and wrote: *12 pencils. Total, six cents.* "Did you put down the amount you owe me?"

"Oh, I forgot," he said. "It's four cents." He wrote down: *4 cents.*

"No, put down *ten cents received.* Then you automatically know how much you owe me. Now where are my pencils?"

"Twelve red pencils to go," the clerk called to the stock boy a few feet away, who seemed much more confident of his role and came forth in no time with the order. The harried clerk took time out to tear off the duplicate copy and place the piece of carbon paper under his next order in preparation for his new customer.

"Margot, you are the bookkeeper for the week—please come up to the board and write out the records you've kept while I go greet a visitor. Hello, I'm Rae," the teacher said warmly. "Welcome to the sevens."

"Thank you. I'm Ellen."

"Have you had a chance to see our store in operation?"

"Yes, I watched the first transaction of the day."

"This is a big day for Christopher. It's the first time he's felt ready to assume the responsibility of chief clerk, and he's still very unsure of himself. He's never wanted to be anything but stock boy up 'til now. Of course every child must learn to assume the responsibility of being in charge, even if it takes a while."

"Is the store open all day?"

"Just for one hour each morning. After a year of Play City, we feel the children are ready for the real world, and this is their first introduction. That's why we use real money."

"Who made the, uh, initial investment, so to speak?"

"Well, of course all the money comes from the fund the parents contribute for the children's school supplies. In Play City toy money is used for the purchase of theatre tickets and taxi rides and even for opening bank accounts."

"I gather that the store is a way of teaching the children arithmetic."

"Yes, that's one of its purposes, although the children work with numbers in Play City. It's here they have responsibility for the first time, and they know that the accounts are expected to come even each week. That's what the class is working on now, tracing a discrepancy in the bookkeeping. Also, the store serves a real purpose—it takes care of the distribution of supplies. As a matter of fact, that's why it was started. The office didn't have time or room to handle such things, and Nellie hit upon the brilliant idea that the children take over the job. After Play City we don't give them any job that doesn't serve a genuine purpose. Our kids would know if they were being fooled. We even pay them a wage."

"And where does that come from?"

"That, too, comes out of the parents' fund for supplies. As far as traditional learning goes, the most important thing about store is the introduction to words. I don't think we have a single child who ever misspells *receive*. Of course, we don't care too much about spelling, but it *is* funny that our children all know how to spell a word that gives others such difficulty."

"What about reading?"

"Well . . . reading is one of our real problems—or should I say, one of the real problems for our parents who tend to panic—because reading is taught at age 6 in the public schools, and here we don't even *attempt* to teach it until 7. We consider ourselves lucky to have squeezed in an extra year of firsthand knowledge unhampered by the necessity of books. If it weren't for the parents and the pressures they put on us, I don't think we'd ever bother with books and other vicarious means of learning."

"I hate to sound stuffy, but what happens with colleges?"

"You don't sound stuffy at all, my dear, you sound just like one of the parents. That is the first question they ask, except they have to worry about high schools too. 'How will my boy ever get into Harvard?' Suppose he didn't and became a carpenter or made leather shoes, as one of our best alumni is now doing in a small town in Vermont? But of course parents get very upset when you tell them that, so we *do* teach reading. But in our own way. And with time, parents learn to put up with us because they see their kids are happy here."

"Yes, I've been struck by that. They do seem to enjoy coming here."

"Of course, we can't take all the credit. Some of the homes are such horrors that any place which respected the rights of children would be a welcomed sanctuary. You needn't make a religion out of it as we do here."

"Getting back to this reading matter, how do the children learn?"

"Actually, it all works out well—and some even go on to Harvard and become corporation lawyers."

"Those, of course, are your failures!"

"Ah, you've caught on, I see! Let me explain a little more. The sixes explore the city—which leads them into an exploration of travel routes and even some history about trading. I don't think you'll find a 6-year-old who can't tell you why the St. Lawrence Seaway was better than some other route for fur or whatever. And of course when they start trading themselves as in the store, they begin to see the necessity of knowing not only numbers but how to spell words. They must write up orders and receipts as well as make change. So that leads us into a study of the ancient civilizations who first started making numbers and letters. Sometimes the kids get so carried away with learning that on occasion I've found it necessary to pull them back into the real world. It's all fine and dandy for a child to start to do research into how the ancient Chinese dynasties kept written records . . ."

"But not if he can't read!"

"I see you're really fixated on reading—which is not unusual for most educated people. Why don't you go visit the

Post Office, one of the most valuable places a child can work? And, Ellen, I'd like to talk to you some more, so do drop back when you've finished seeing the rest of our place."

"Where *is* the Post Office?"

"Oh my, I forgot to say. It's in Forest South, which you get to by crossing the yard. Just head for the second floor— you can't miss it. And don't forget to drop by again. We've hardly gotten to know each other."

The Post Office contained several sections. One was labeled "Stamps for Outer Routes," another, "Stamps for Inner Routes." I inquired of the child behind the Outer Route counter what was the difference between her stamps and the Inner Routes' ones.

"Our stamps are for letters going outside the school."

"You mean, real postage stamps?"

"Well, all stamps are *real*. That is, no letter can be delivered anywhere, inner or outer, unless it's properly stamped. Excuse me please," she said, as a boy approached and asked to have a manila envelope weighed. "How far is it going?"

"From Forest South two to Forest North three."

"That will be a four-cent stamp," said the clerk and pulled out a beautifully printed stamp, which she handed over and which the boy put on.

"I would also like to buy a stamped envelope for outer routes."

"That's at Counter Two," she said, pointing to the adjacent desk. "Are you new or something?" she then asked the boy.

"No, but I never ran the inner route before, just the outer one," he answered.

"What's the Parcel Post service?" I asked, pointing toward another section.

"That's a special route we run for parents who have messages to deliver to us. It's actually our busiest service, except at Christmas, when the outer routes get pretty busy too. Then we have to hire additional workers and even do work overtime. Of course we're paid extra if we work overtime, so it's not so bad."

"May I ask what your salary is?"

"You mean our wage."

"Yes."

"It comes out to about fifteen cents a month."

"I see," I said.

"If you just put in one hour a month, that's the wage—fifteen cents an hour. Of course, if you work more, you make more, but most of us just work one hour a month delivering letters."

"This is really exciting to see," I said. "Now I know where all the pretty printed work that I've seen around comes from."

"Glad you like us; I didn't get your name," the taller of the two women said.

"Ellen."

"Ellen, I'm Jo, and my partner here is Annie. Annie has the tens, whom she prepares for me."

"I'll say. Unless they come well prepared, I don't hear the end of it."

"Annie and I live together, so she can't get away with much."

"You mean I can't get away from *you,* Jo."

"Now would you really want to, Annie?"

Annie cleared her throat. "Our main job is almost invisible at this point. We just see that everything is kept humming. The printing presses are so exciting that once the children master them, there's little work for us."

"Oh, Jo, don't make us sound so *lazy.*"

"Well go ahead, Annie, and tell your own tale."

"All right. With your permission, I'll give an accounting of what one-half of this partnership attempts to do."

"I want it made clear that each half of this partnership succeeds in what it attempts to do."

"Okay. Now hush, Jo. This is a two-year plan, Ellen. I handle the first part, although in effect we really do work together, Jo and I. But I'm in charge of teaching the tens how to print on paper, which leads us quite naturally into a study of manuscripts and the Middle Ages."

"Children love that period which *I* was taught were the Dark Ages," I said.

"They do. But we must avoid certain things, Ellen. One of the reasons children love the Middle Ages is because of all the knights in shining armor and other romantic nonsense they get from God knows where."

"From musicals and TV," said Jo.

"Well, King Arthur didn't exactly discourage it either, which is why we don't have our kids read those kind of books. We want them to know those romantic trappings weren't the entire story, and that there were others living in that period whose lives were far from glamorous. When we have plays our children start out wanting to be knights, but wind up playing serfs and mean masters—which of course is a lot more accurate."

"And also more exciting," Jo said.

"True enough. But let's tell Ellen about our curriculum, if you'll pardon the term. Once they learn about manuscripts and hand printing, it's hard to avoid print and books, all of which leads us to a study of the Renaissance. We have guilds and journeymen, and the elevens even have the tens as apprentices. By the end of the year they actually pass their craft onto those following them. It all works out very well."

"It certainly sounds that way. What do the tens do for their school job?"

"Oh there's no lack of work for them," Annie continued. "First of all, they're in charge of the printing of the library cards, which are hand-done according to a very unique system devised by Henry—Henrietta, that is, our librarian. Since the school uses no books for the classroom, the library's an important place. Once he starts to read, each child must spend an hour a day there, picking out books he likes. I have one youngster who's teaching himself Arabic because he's so excited about Middle Eastern music."

"Do tell Ellen that this particular youngster can barely read English."

"Is that what we care about? I'd much rather have a child who teaches himself Arabic on his own than one who can diagram a sentence from the *New York Times* according to its grammatical structure, the way we used to do."

"And how many centuries ago was that, Annie?"

"I don't know what's gotten into Jo this morning."

"It's your overly done scrambled eggs that have gotten into me this morning, if I may have the pleasure of being honest."

"May I have the pleasure of interrupting?"

"Yes, of course, Ellen. What?"

"What kind of books do the children read on their own?"

"Mainly diaries and journals and all the letters they can get hold of. Whatever's closest to firsthand information."

"And the juiciest too, Annie. Admit it."

"But juicy or no, our children have no fear of libraries and card catalogues, since they printed them when they were tens. They're absolutely fearless where other children tense up, like the first time they're in a library and they have to find a book on their own."

"Which would be an invaluable aid in research, if only they could read, as well," put in Jo.

"Jo, have you ever found a child anywhere who enjoys sitting still and idle for any length of time?"

"Yes, one who's ill. I'm sure you've heard it from Nell, from Dewey, from Rae, so why not hear it from me? After all, there would be no music without repetition, would there, my dear? First theme number one. The moment we impose second-hand information from an authority—either a teacher or a book; doesn't much matter, neither one is from the world directly—we begin to waste the child, and his innate desire to learn starts to wither away. We can see that right here. But there comes a time in a child's young life when his parents want him to be prepared to take a part in the real world. Since we do not own the child entirely, we must begin to take him out of the real world and set him on his way for the ersatz road his parents call reality. And that includes reading."

"Of course, some children never take to it," Annie added. "After experiencing meaningful work, who would want to sit in a chair still and quiet reading?"

"See that boy over there who's so busy with the press?" Jo pointed to a youngster who was handling one of the machines. "He knows more about these presses than any other child, but he refuses to read. So when we have reading sessions at the end of the day—which the children are free to skip, as with any other activity—Edward sits in the back drawing. Now most of our children do *something* while I read, that is, they don't just sit there nailed down to their seats, but they manage to follow the story, even when they skip reading for a couple of days. But not our Edward. He is so absorbed in his drawing that I try to read softly enough to exclude him."

"You see, Ellen? Jo's really the biggest rebel of us all. She even has to rebel against her own rebellion every now and then."

"Now don't expose me all at once, Annie, just because you know me so well."

At the end of my second day of observation, Rae saw me about to leave school and caught my arm.

"Aren't you coming to the weekly?"

"Uh, weekly what?"

"Oh dear, I keep on forgetting that you're new. The

weekly's a conference—I guess you would call it that, if **you** wanted to give it an official-sounding name."

"I didn't hear anything about it, Rae. Where's it held?"

"Right in the apartment. We meet in our apartment, that is, Nellie's, but it's really for all of us anytime we want to relax or whenever we think a child needs to get away from the school atmosphere."

"Where is it?"

"Right in Forest North. We have the entire third floor. That's where Nellie lives."

"Oh, I was confused because you said when a child wants to get away from the school. . . ."

"No, I meant get away from the other kids or the other teachers, not the building itself."

I followed Rae to the third floor, where there was a locked orange door with a sign printed on it: "Private. Permission necessary to enter."

The only way Nellie's apartment differed from her office was that little children didn't constantly storm in, only adults. Otherwise it had the same crowded, cozy atmosphere and overflowed with half-completed hand-crafted objects. The furniture was old and comfortable. Dewey, more oafish-looking than before, came in and plopped down into the largest, most sunken chair and declared it hers for the evening as if she had just conquered a mountain.

"Has someone sent out for the food?"

"Why don't I call up the Shanghai and have them send up some shrimps and things? Then no one will have to fuss."

"But what about Annie? She doesn't like fish."

"We'll order a chicken dish too."

"Dewey, you do the calling and I'll do the ordering, since I know exactly what Annie can eat and what she can't. How's that?"

Throughout all the ploppings and declarations I felt uncomfortable. I didn't know what to do. Should I offer to pay, suggest a dish, or just sit quietly and have the others think I was ill? Everyone was so busy pretending to be at ease that relaxation threatened to take over the tiny apartment by force.

"Jo, what would you do with a father who insists on taking his son to the circus?" asked Annie.

"Whose father's that?"

"Ivan's. I told him the school has nothing against circuses per se. I used to love the little one that came to our town and can still remember the acrobatics I saw. But I was about three feet away from the ring, which was in the middle of a meadow, and not in some godawful smoke-filled place which has the nerve to call itself a garden."

"Well, did he understand you when you told him why we oppose the circus?"

"Hard to say. You know he was polite, but I don't think he has any plans to exchange the tickets."

"I've always thought it's the mothers who are our enemies, but sometimes I wonder."

"No, it *is* the mothers, Jo, if you overlook one thing with the fathers—that magic baseball ring. There's something about a baseball game that fathers consider inviolate. You'd think we were stealing their wives or something from the way they carry on. And there, too, they just don't understand that our objection is not to the game itself."

"Although it is highly structured and unspontaneous," said Jo.

"And boring as well, if you want to know my opinion."

"Besides, it's crowds all over again, no chance for any individual response, everyone getting excited or miserable at the same thing; even singing the national anthem together over a loudspeaker. But I've given up on baseball. I don't know what to say about the circus."

"Dewey, did you call up for the food?"

"I thought Jo was going to do that."

"Jo, on your feet, I'm getting hungry," said Annie.

"What about some real problems, gals, like what are we going to do about our gangsters?"

"How many are there?" Nellie asked.

"Well, according to Adam there are three."

"And they are all in the twelves, are they? That's a bully-ish age. I really think that it is our job to instruct the others how to deal with gangsters. Gangsters couldn't flourish if we didn't have a weak group."

"I have an idea," Rae said. "Why don't we hire someone to teach the kids boxing?"

"A fine idea, but where is the money to come from?" Nellie asked.

"Isn't Conrad leaving?"

"Conrad's the science teacher, Ellen," Rae whispered.

"Yes, I think so, but he wasn't sure."

"Why don't we use his salary for a professional boxing instructor?"

"Magnificent. I applaud that decision."

"Conrad may not leave."

"Then why don't we each sacrifice a little bit of our salary to hire someone for a short time? I think it's worth it. How about it?"

"This is the first moment of silence since we've started," Jo observed. "Shall I take that as a sign of consent?"

"If you find the instructor and take care of the whole thing, I'm willing to along with it," Nellie said. "How about the rest? Well, that takes care of that. And just in time; there's the bell." Nellie got up to open the door.

"One more thing, though," Jo said. "I don't think we should let the three who've been clobbering the others take part in the lessons."

"What'll you tell them, since everything is voluntary?"

"I think I'll tell them that since they're such good fighters, there's no need for them to waste their time with an instructor. No problem whatsoever."

"When will we have the lessons?"

"How about during Yard?" Annie asked. "It seems the kids have been unresourceful out there lately."

"I've noticed that too, but I hate to have Yard associated with fighting," Nellie said, entering the room with several paper buckets of Chinese food.

"Why not? You think the animals in the jungle went without fighting? Aggression is a perfectly natural thing. If it weren't, I wouldn't have suggested it in the first place," said Jo.

"Here—let me get some plates," Rae said. "Follow me, Ellen, and I'll show you the kitchen. You might want to come up here some time and make yourself something to eat."

"You know, I live right down the street."

"Even so. You'll see—it can be very cozy. Do you live alone, Ellen?"

"Yes."

"All the more reason to get to know this place. But I don't want to press you," Rae said as we entered the kitchen. "This is it—everything you'll ever need is right in this little room. Nellie bakes her own breads here. I kid her all the time about that. Just like having babies—baking bread. Don't you think?"

"It *is* kind of domestic, if that's what you mean."

"*Kind* of? Here, take a handful of silver and I'll bring in the plates."

"How did your play go this week, Dewey?" Nellie asked as she spooned out some rice on the plates Rae handed her.

"I can't claim complete success, but there were a few triumphs. You know little Amy, the self-righteous six who's always worrying about whether everyone's working as hard as he should? Well, we finally got her to play the role of a submissive factory hand who listens to orders screeched at her all day long. You should have seen her. At first she still continued to work as hard as can be. But when the script had her clean the floors and mop up and do things she considered beneath her intelligence, she really began to sulk. She couldn't stand the part which was just perfect for her."

"I'll know it was perfect if she stops criticizing the others," Jo commented. "But go on with the triumphs."

"Well, Timmy surprised me too. He's always been such a little lamb. But when we made him play the part of the union organizer, he really *did* lead the workers."

"Any luck with Leon this time?"

"Absolutely none. I tried desperately to get him to be a

worker instead of an intellectual, but he remained detached and superior the whole time, except for when he could throw some facts in someone's face. Never once really identified with the role of a worker. Why don't we make him the problem for this weekly? Unless someone has another child in mind?"

"Anyone object to the choice of Leon? Good. We'll return to him after we finish with the more general things."

"Annie, how's Paul doing?"

"Paul is now well launched into color. He doesn't paint everything in purples and blacks anymore, and I think he's beginning to develop a sense of self-confidence. Of course, he still has an unfinished birdhouse in the woodshop, but I haven't reminded him. It's so good to see him interested in freer kinds of things with no obvious function. Anyway, there's absolutely no chance that he won't go back and finish it."

"Responsibility's his whole problem. It'd be a pleasure to see that child really let go."

"Well, he's coming along fine in the lunchroom," Annie said. "He no longer insists on eating like a tiny gentleman. He's finally spurned his fork and napkin. I even saw him rolling his spaghetti the other day with his fingers and playing with it before he finally ate it."

"That kind of substitute masturbation can't be very satisfying, but it certainly shows progress. I don't think we ever had a more repressed child!"

"Except for Leon, of course. He's still painting pictures with grass below and sky above and houses and trees in a straight line."

"Oh yes, Leon. I consider him in a category of his own," Nellie said. "You know I've always had great pity for the so-called *bright* child. Leon is a walking proof of why I feel that way. Of course, we mustn't be too hard on him; it's the parents who made him the way he is. I sometimes think we never should have accepted him, even though he has the highest I.Q. in the class. All he wants is *information*."

"He actually reads encyclopedias, which may be why."

"The saddest part is that the other kids despise him."

"Well, who wouldn't? Children are the best test of character. He's always spouting some fact in their face, and they couldn't care less. And he corrects them constantly."

"Of course he's not as open when it comes to his own mistakes. They never happen in math or science; he sees to that. But I watched him in Yard one day when he was playing a game, and every time he missed the ball, he blamed the thrower or the yard or something, so he would be in the clear."

"Why do you think the other kids put up with that?"

"I asked them that myself just the other day. The game was over, and I had Leon go on an errand so I could find out why they let him get away with all those excuses. They said, 'He needs them. That's the only way he can face up because he can't play ball.'"

"And in rhythms he's afraid even to somersault on a mat," Dewey said.

"Well just look at the *father,* if you want an idea. Pouchy, stooped over, bags under his eyes. An accountant."

"Any parent is going to cause trouble just by being a parent, but at least the creative ones understand us better."

"That's what I mean," Nellie said. "It's not really Leon's fault that he's such a pompous little ass. After all, he spends more time at home than here. And it's the kind of home where at six o'clock the mother comes in and says, 'Stop what you are doing, Leon, dinner is being served.' Somewhere she read that order is good for a child, but of course she didn't learn that interrupting a child is about the *worst* thing you can do. I wonder how *she* would like to be told to leave in the middle of a play? That's what we should do with parents like that, interrupt *their* play time."

"Oh don't be silly. You don't think the house is really orderly? Dinner time is when the chaos begins. If you want proof, just look at what a picky eater Leon is."

"Naturally. Any child whose creativity is stifled is going to hate the sensual activities."

"And then Leon's mother fights with Leon's father over what is the best way to handle Leon."

"His analyst certainly seems like an ass. I called him the other day and he refused to give out any information. Said it was between Leon and himself, and he couldn't 'violate their privacy.'"

"The parents have a fetish about privacy too. Noticed how modest Leon is about undressing in rhythms? And of course the other kids never include him in their sex sessions. I guess you do have to feel sorry for a boy who's so obnoxious. I know Maggie can't stand him."

"Well, at least she won't have to put up with him for a month. Maggie is leaving tonight for Greece, you know."

"Since when does Maggie bolt off just like that?"

"She's going to check up on a question that arose while

teaching the twelves about Greece, one she feels can't be answered in any other way. I think it's to our credit that teachers here do things like that."

"Indeed," Jo put in, " 'tis a credit to Forest, but what about her poor little twelves? Are they to accompany her in her research?"

"Well, I guess this is the time to introduce Ellen, who's been sitting in on all this, thinking Lord only knows what."

"Oh, Nellie, since when do we need formal introductions? Most of us have met Ellen anyway. As a matter of fact, I've already shown her every cup and saucer in your kitchen."

"Does she talk, Rae?"

"Dewey, that is a *most* ungracious comment."

"You don't take me seriously do you—Ellen, is it?"

"Right."

"Ellen's been looking us over to see if she would like to take Maggie's place for the time being."

"Do you like what you've seen?"

"That's a direct one, Jo."

"I'd like to find that out."

"Would you like to teach here for the month?"

"Yes."

"Good," Rae said, taking my hand in hers. "I'm happy you're going to be here, Ellen; we need to know one another better."

Sunday

Dear Canelli,

   Am lost in Forest, where strange creatures exist. Everyone here is very physically active and possibly even predatory, which is appealing to one who has always thought of school as a reasonably quiet, orderly place—you know, a little like a library, except there's an adult up front. And now all this is being questioned. Sitting still at Forest is considered a symptom of illness.

Here, even though everyone says there is no set philosophy, I have been bombarded with little talks about "what Forest stands for," which always means what Forest is against. *And the seductive part is that Forest is against all the things we should be against—factories, smog, and everything large and anonymous in city life. Yet the school exists in the city, and the kids are so citified that it is almost sickening. Forest is filled with contradictions, which is why it's intriguing.*

Part of their philosophy is to plan all curriculum around a work program. Their play store sells supplies which the kids use. All you need is one authentic detail to make kids believe in it—like the receipt pad with its carbon paper that the "clerk" has to slide between each new sale after he tears off the duplicate copy. There's something magical about the carbon paper; it suddenly makes the whole "transaction" real.

The only trouble is that reality no longer is real. How many little stores are there left in the world? I mean, shouldn't the kids be learning how to stick things in computers if they want to imitate adult society? Everyone at Forest may be deluded that the school is the Real World. But that's what happens when you spend too much time in little worlds. I'm trying like mad to hold off judgment, to look and see for myself as Nellie has advised me a million times to do.

Just a mention of Forest's triumph—the printing presses

which the 11-year-olds (henceforth to be called the elevens) run. They are real machines which hum and buzz and do everything that machines should do. They even lop fingers off sloppy workers, although that happened only once. The elevens wear workmen's aprons to protect their dungarees, but their faces and hands get soiled all over with printers' ink.

This excites the teachers very much—uptight types that they are, who pick the chapters from Freud that tickle them. Like having an opportunity to play with dirt since "our culture doesn't let you mess around with the body's very first creative product," which is why everyone feels compelled to make piles of money. Life at Forest is exceedingly anal. I mean there's so much talk about not being "tight" or "rigid," about not having to make money or being concerned with success. Naturally, order and neatness are the sins, just as lack of them were at Andrews. Do you suppose it is the opposite side of the same coin?

At Andrews not even scrap paper was wasted, but kids at Forest are encouraged to throw things away, encouraged not to count their supplies out carefully, encouraged to drop things, start over again, leave what doesn't interest them. You get some sense of this when you see the teachers. If it weren't for villagey touches like dark stockings and handmade jewelry, they sure would resemble stern headmistress types whom they all had when they went to school. They're mostly in their early fifties, but dress like old-fashioned schoolgirls (That is, like boys). You know the type, Canelli, the aging suffragette: lots of energy, lots of vitality, and "piles" of anger. They all have short-cropped hair—not mannish as much as boyish bobs

they don't have to fuss with. Only one is soft looking, and her
name is Rae. She has been the friendliest of the lot to me.

Whereas Andrews held faculty conferences with the regu-
larity of good bowel movements, Forest holds sheer purges
where crap gets thrown about or waddled in. After openly
dissecting various disturbed kids the greatest venom was re-
served for an all too recognizable type—an ex-public school
kid who's overly brainy and underly physical, which he com-
pensates for by throwing facts at everyone. Now the private
school mentality strikes again. I really wonder if there is a
single school besides the Yeshiva that is free of this combina-
tion delicious-malicious gossip. The only thing in favor of
Forest is that there is no attempt to cover it up with politeness,
parliamentary procedure, or any other camouflage employed
by Andrews.

Now, Canelli, I must end for the moment, and prepare my-
self for tomorrow when I have my first class, the twelves.

As soon as I set foot inside my classroom, a kid with long
bangs looked up from under his hair and said, "Where's Maggie?"

"She left for Greece to do some research," I answered.

"Who are you?"

"I'm Maggie's replacement while she's gone."

"Yep, she's the one from the yard," Adam said.

"What's your name again?"

"Ellen."

"Shit," said the first boy, "I'm leaving." And so he did.
I didn't panic yet; that was only one gone, and there were

still fourteen more before the class became an empty room. Then a reassuring voice. "Don't worry, Kirk is very moody. He'll be back in a few minutes." Exactly on time, Kirk returned.

"Just ignore me, just ignore me. Don't take me seriously," he muttered, interrupting another kid who was asking where I taught previously. I mentioned Andrews.

"Oh, that's one of those regular kind of places, right, Ellen?"

"Yeah, it's like my old school," Kirk answered for me. "I used to go to Greenwich Academy, and there it really stinks. I mean they don't give a damn about the kids underneath. They just pretend to, so the parents keep on paying."

"I used to go to public school, and they don't care there either," a boy with carrot-colored hair said.

"That's Leon," Kirk informed me. "No one can stand him in this class except me."

"Hey, Kirk, why don't you shut up?" a strange voice said. So far I was just following faces and words. Now Kirk was up and off again. "Don't hurry back, Kirk." Kirk returned even faster this time, still muttering his speech: "Don't take me seriously. I'm very confused. Even though I'm extremely bright and sensitive, most of my teachers can't take me. I'm too much, I know. I need love too badly or something. Anyway, I'm all screwed up and not even my psychiatrist has much hope for me. That's why I like Leon. He's a mess too. I mean he needs attention even more than I do!"

"But you certainly seem more successful in demanding it," I said. "I mean, how come you're telling me all about your psychiatrist and stuff?"

"I told you why. Because I like to call attention to myself. But just don't take me seriously, or you'll be in trouble. Maggie is the only one who knows how to take me. When's she coming back?"

"In about a month."

"Does she have a phone in Greece? I think I'll call her," and out he walked for the third time. I tried to take advantage of his absence and asked the class what they had been studying.

"Greece."

"Ancient or modern?"

"We don't learn dates here. Maggie doesn't care about them."

Now I abandoned all temporal concerns, only to be told it was time for rhythms. "So long, Ellen," and out the class skipped, leaving me with four blank walls.

"Hey, want to come?" a boy called out as he eyed me sitting forlornly on a table top.

"Sure, where is it?"

"In the gym."

"And where's that?"

"On the top floor. Got to hurry. Dewey doesn't like it if we're late."

I prepared to rush out and follow him. But I didn't know what to grab; everyone looked so free of baggage. The fact that Forest had no required books helped the kids to have lighter loads. I lugged my big teacher pocketbook with me and ran after the kids, but I was at a decided disadvantage in my sling-back shoes, mounting steps painted alternately orange and green up to the gym, where I felt ready to collapse with zigzag dizziness. But not the kids. They were already unrolling mats and starting to cartwheel while Dewey stood nearby, imposing a strict rhythm with a yardstick she used like the arm of a metronome, on some dreamy Debussy-like music that a faggy guy was playing on a piano. The children rolled over one after another with ease and grace, and Kirk managed to slip in a tiny pirouette after his somersault, which caused Dewey to skip a beat. She quickly got back into rhythm just in time for Leon, who hesitated as he approached the mat.

"Stop the music, Pierre," Dewey called out to the piano player, which brought all movement to a halt. All eyes were focused on Leon. He was now standing on his head while Dewey tried to get his long and lanky limbs to relax.

"Stiff as this ruler," she observed, before rapping him lightly on his behind. "Go limp with your body, Leon, like you have collapsed." Dewey waited. But it was like defrosting a frozen turkey in five minutes. Leon remained undefrosted. "Come here, Chris. Take hold of this leg. What does it feel like? Stiff, right?" Chris nodded. "Okay, I want you to do with the leg you are holding" (which was Leon's, of course) "what I do with mine. We're going to give Leon a massage to relax him, since he can't do it on his own."

Leon's face reddened now so that it was almost as bright as his hair. But it was hard to know whether the red was due to shame or just the accumulation of blood responding to the laws of gravity. "Pierre, some sleepy-type music," Dewey called out as she begins to stroke Leon's leg, starting first with his toes. "Now with me, Chris, up and down, smoothly and evenly. And you, Leon, stop that squirming; it's essential that you learn how to relax. Your muscles are in knots, they're so tense. If only you could feel them for yourself." As Dewey, followed hesitantly by Chris began to close in on the crotch, Leon relaxed completely. He fainted.

"Enough now, Chris. Leon will come to in a minute. It's his way of giving up control, the only way some people can let go." As soon as Dewey stopped touching Leon, he revived. "Time for Greece now," Dewey announced.

Leon stood up and said, "But Dewey, we've been doing Greece all along, because it was the Greeks who said a sound mind needs a sound body."

"That's it, Leon," said Kirk. "Don't let the hag beat you. She can get you with her hands but you can get her back with your brain." And now Kirk, the beautiful elfin boy with dark long hair and light blue eyes, went over to Leon and congratulated him, slapping him on the back like a company president who had just promoted a junior executive.

By now the mats had been rolled up, some children had gotten out Greek instruments, and others were starting to depict Greek myths through mime and dance while Pierre played Greek music.

"Hold those torches high," Dewey said to the kids whose arms were grasping the air. I stood aside admiring the imaginativeness and freeness of movement. The kids were so good at this sort of thing I could actually recognize some of the myths they acted out. While they were working on their own, Dewey came over to me and took a look at my sheer nylon stockings in their sling-back shoes. "It's not at all necessary to dress like this, Ellen. As a matter of fact, we feel it's a bad influence on the girls who are starting to yearn for frills and other clothing that interferes with free movement. We try to de-emphasize all that, including the difference between boys and girls which our society makes such a fetish of."

I looked at Dewey in her simple steel gray wool skirt, her tailored shirt and knee socks.

An historian or social scientist would be amused by the activity following Ancient Civilization: Contemporary Reality. All music stopped. "Who wants to do the first skit?" Dewey asked. Almost every hand went up. Dewey chose three children and the rest formed a circle around them. "Let's see who's the first to guess what's happening." The trio consulted in the center like some shrunken football squad and finally started to act out a scene.

After a few minutes I began to piece together what was happening. Dewey jumped up and down as the family crisis culminated in one child sneaking out an imaginary door. I couldn't figure out whether it was the lover or spouse fleeing, but the kids seemed to comprehend perfectly. Other acts followed, and although the actors changed, the stories all concerned family crises and all elicited jumps of joy from Dewey. She was especially elated when something "juicy" was executed and a kid guessed correctly what it was.

"They're such little social realists," she said to me. "If you want to know what's going on in their homes, just watch these playlets. We learn more from the spontaneous behavior of children than from any other source. That's why we don't hold the usual parent conferences unless they're requested. Children are far more reliable sources of information about what is going on at home." For all her appreciation of the kids' liberation and spontaneity, Dewey couldn't overcome her own traditional school days where games contained three elements—competition, physical exercise, and shame. Even her "playlets" became competitive when she picked the best one at the end of the activity, "that is, the one truest to life."

Right after the best one was chosen, an army of little children stormed into the gym. Here come the fours. "The fours are here, Pierre."

Pierre raced to the piano, and the first little four to invade the gym cried out, "Play some creepy music today, Pierre."

"No," said another, "I want wild music."

"Please, please, loves, not all at once. My goodness, Pierre just can't play more than one thing at one time, *mes petits,* can I?" Again he started playing his sleepy music. But the children didn't mind, and soon each twelve was taking a four for a partner and everyone was dancing. Not since I saw the Hasidic men dancing in the streets of Williamsburg had I been so touched by spontaneous tenderness—especially as shown by boys, and without any self-consciousness. The whole sight restored my enthusiasm for "rhythms."

"This is how we teach the older children responsibility," Dewey said. "First a twelve dances with a four, and then the older child takes the little one down to the cafeteria where he serves him milk and cookies." Dewey didn't know that she knocked all the joy from the scene when she inserted a moral.

How could I have ever felt challenged at Andrews, an absolute sanctuary by comparison?

"Okay, kids, let's get to work on Greece today."

"Oh no, Ellen. Only Maggie can teach us that."

"Yeah, have you ever lived there?"

"No," I admitted.

"Then how can you know about it?"

"But Maggie didn't live there hundreds of years ago, and certainly you must study something about ancient Greece."

"Bullshit. You haven't lived there, and you're just covering up. Phoniness. That really gets me mad, man. I'm leaving."

"Wait up, Kirk," another chimed in, "I'll go with you."

"Listen, maybe you'd all like to leave."

"Yeah, come on."

"No, I don't want to leave."

"Me either. Let's let Kirk and whoever else wants to, go and we'll stay with you, Ellen."

"Frankly, I feel very funny sitting here when people just get up and walk out. I mean, if you were here, I think you'd feel the same way. You don't even have to be a teacher, just the only stranger in a group where everyone else knows each other. How would you feel if people started to walk out whenever you started to talk?"

"Lousy, damned lousy. I'm never walking out again."

"Kirk! When did you get back?"

"By now you should know that I never stay out for any length of time. It's just that you're doing things all wrong, and it's very painful for me to see. That's really why I left. I mean, I know you're trying and all, but you're just not getting there."

"Why don't you help me?"

"Me? Help you? That's a joke. Wait a second, I have to laugh. It's too much. I need so much help myself, you can't depend on me for guidance. That's a real scream. I think I have to leave for that."

"I thought you weren't going to leave anymore."

"No, I lied. I told you not to trust anything I say or do."

So Kirk left, and I turned to the remainder. "I'm still not used to this sort of thing, kids. Why don't you all go off to some workshop now and let me think for a while about things?"

"Where should we go?"

"Wherever the others go when they walk out. Don't you have your own work activity?"

"We're supposed to be working on toys for the 'Never Say Shit' Toy Company."

"The what?"

"The 'Never Say Shit' Toy Company. That's the name of our business."

"I didn't know the twelves made toys."

"Yeah, we have the company where we're supposed to make 'em."

"What do you learn from that?"

"We're *supposed* to learn about management and organization. I guess you'd call it economics."

"You don't sound too enthusiastic."

"Shit, who cares about making toys? Anyway, we did all that when we were six. It's really the same thing, except now we have a company and we make believe we have management and labor problems, but it's all phony. I mean, this school is great up until now, because all the little make-believe worlds really do prepare you for the printing presses, and with them you can do something. But after that everything is a bore."

"And babyish, besides."

"Have you spoken to Nellie about this?"

"Sure."

"What does she say?"

"Nellie's so hung up on jobs as the center of the school that she can't say anything. I mean, she can't see it."

"That's the real reason everyone is so bored and keeps on walking in and out. We don't have enough to do that we like. At least with Maggie we learn something."

"It's obvious that the 'So-and-So' Toy Company has to go. Why don't you give me until tomorrow to think about something to replace it? Now I want to wander around the workshops and see how the other kids spend their time when they're on their own. Maybe that'll inspire me."

"Want us to show you around?"

"Sure. What workshop is that one at the foot of the stairs?"

"That's art. Willie's not there now."

"Who's Willie?"

"The art teacher."

"What in heaven's name is that little girl over there doing?"

"She's drawing a dot on each piece of paper and then crumpling it up and throwing it away."

"Gee whiz, Michael, thanks a lot. I mean *why* is she putting a dot on each paper or why is she being allowed to throw away forty pieces of paper?"

"The whole idea is, it's better to waste materials than human creativity, so we can use as many papers as we want."

"But she's not doing anything very creative with the papers."

"Okay, maybe it's not so creative, but maybe it'll *lead* to something creative. I mean, how can you tell?"

"I guess I'm prejudiced that way, about waste. It just seems wrong to me."

"Listen," Michael said, "when you've spent enough time in art, come next door to the nature room. That's where I'll be. You know where it is?"

"Sure. It's where they have that insane bird locked up." I continued on.

"Hi. Aren't you the clerk I met in the Post Office?"

"Yes, I answered some of your questions."

"You did. But I never learned your name."

"It's Nina."

"And I'm Ellen. I've been watching you draw. Would you like some help?"

"Sure."

"Look at the ears you've put down. They're sitting on top of the head."

"Where should they be?"

"Why don't you look at my ears? Or better still, touch your own and see where they are. That's it. Where do they start and end in relation to the other features?"

"Ooh, I never realized they were so low."

"Most people don't when they draw."

"You're right. They start at the eyes and end at the nose."

"Now put your hand back on your ear and tell me what you feel behind it."

"My neck."

"But look where you have it on your paper."

"I wonder why."

"All kids seem to draw the neck that way too, as if it started under the face and was much skinnier."

"My God, isn't it ridiculous!"

"Well, it is if you want to draw a realistic looking face."

"I do. I have to change that. What else, Ellen? It still doesn't look right."

"Why don't you get a model and look at her face."

"Can I use you?"

"Sure."

"I know. It's the eyes that are off. I made mine much too far apart. That's terrific. Thank you."

"Hey, what's going on here? I don't think we met before."

"I'm Ellen. I was just observing some of your students."

"I don't mind observing, but that's not all you were doing. I heard you telling Nina how to make a face, which upsets me no end because I teach my kids that there is no standard way to do anything in the world. The only way that ever makes sense is the one that springs from within. Then I come along and hear you talking about where *this* is and where *that* is. Where would Picasso and Chagall be if they worried about making faces look like real faces? And anyway, every face, even real ones, are different. My features are different from yours just the way Chinese faces are different from whites'. So if you want to observe my shop, okay. But don't go around giving out this kind of stuff. I really get pissed off when someone takes over my class."

"I'm sorry. I didn't intend to interfere."

"I'm sorry too. I just had to blow my top, because if there's anything I can't stand it's conformity. In art, especially. This should be the freest area of them all. Now what did you say your name is?"

"Ellen."

"Good, I'm Willie. Let's just forget the fuss. Stop by when you want. Are you leaving now?"

"Yes, I have to return to my class."

"Hey, Ellen, we heard you really got it from Willie."

"Don't let it get you down; she's like that with everyone. Very hostile come-on. But when she knows you, she eases up."

"Also, she doesn't like people to hang around her class, no matter how much she denies it."

"How did you kids hear all of this?"

"We were right next door. That's why we came back."

"You mean you felt sorry for me?"

"Yeh. It's hard when you're in a new place, especially here where nobody tells you anything unless you ask."

"You're really very sweet."

"You know, Ellen, it's not so easy for Willie either. She's all alone too."

"You mean because she's Negro?"

"Yes, and the only one at Forest."

"Why is that, in a progressive school like this?"

"I have a Negro stepfather, and that's really rough."

"I forgot your name. Please tell it to me again."

"Lisa. I'm the one with the Negro stepfather."

"Don't complain, Lisa, that's better than mine. My father lives in California, and every winter vacation he makes me fly over to visit just to check up that my mother's been feeding me and all that jazz."

"Hey, Ellen, you should see Lisa's stepfather. He really is dark. Not just Negro, he's black."

"Is he African?"

"Yeah, and he wears these crazy colors all wrapped around."

"He does not, Kirk. Only when my friends come over, because he knows that most Americans think that Africans eat each other and swing from trees and all that kind of stuff."

"That's because Americans are so dumb. We don't know a thing about anything. Nothing. Absolutely nothing. Now take me. . . ."

"Kirk, I've taken enough of you. Let someone else talk."

"What do I know about Africa, if I'm being honest. I've never been there. All I know is what I see on TV, and. . . ."

"And I said to shut up, Kirk, or I'm going to ask you to leave."

"Anyway Kirk knows about Negroes. He lives right in the city."

"I do not. I just know my parents, and I think they're white."

"How about all your maids, Kirk?"

"Let me see. I think they're all white too. But my horse is black."

"I wish I had a black stepfather instead of my own. I mean

he could be any color as long as he were a different person. I really hate his guts and you want to know something? He knows it. I know he knows it, and that just makes it all the worse. If that man calls me 'my son' one more time I'm going to. . . ."

"You're not going to do anything, Michael. You're just talk."

"I am not. I'm going to give him one just like Aki showed us."

"Who's Aki?"

"The new karate instructor. He's teaching us self-defense."

"Like it?"

"No."

"It just teaches you to treat violence with violence."

"Hey, Leon, you better shut up and learn how to defend yourself, because you're the kind who's always going to be picked on. Now take me. No one wants to hurt me be-cause. . . ."

"Kirk, in one more minute I'm going to *kill* you if you don't let others talk."

"Ha, Kirk, she's on to you."

"What were you saying, Leon?"

"I forgot."

"Ellen, I want to say something."

"Go ahead."

"How come we can't just have everyone intermarry and then one day we'd wind up with only one color and there would be no more problems?"

"You're wrong, Lisa, because if you intermarry too much you get idiots."

"How do you know, Michael?"

"Because I saw them. Some royal family. I think it was in Spain. My real father told me about that when he showed me this picture that had a retarded kid. It was really a riot because the kid was all dressed up in these fancy clothes just like the others, but you could see something was wrong with him."

"I thought your father was in California."

"He is, but we flew to Spain one vacation."

"Look, you kids are always getting off the topic. It's worse than listening to a psychiatrist's free association test."

"What's free association, Ellen? I go to a psychiatrist but I don't think I do free associating. We just play darts all the time, and I always beat him because he thinks it's good for me."

Leon was quick with an answer. "Jonathan, free associating means you say whatever comes into your mind without thinking about it. You just talk out whatever you think."

"How do you know, Leon?"

"Never mind how Leon knows. He's right, which is what matters. And if you stop interrupting each other for a minute, we can do a free association exercise. Do you want to? Okay, take out a piece of paper and something to write with."

"Can we use an envelope?"

"I don't see why not."

"Yeah, Shubert composed a whole symphony on one."

"Stop free associating yourself, Kirk, so the whole class can. Okay, has everyone got something?"

"Yes, go ahead, we're ready."

"All right. I'm going to say a phrase and you write down the first image, the first mental picture that you see. Don't think about it; just put down whatever floats into your mind. All set?"

"Yeah."

"Scarlet snow."

"When can we tell you what we wrote?"

"As soon as everyone's finished, Kirk."

"Hurry up, everybody."

Wed'y nite

Canelli dear,

Can you picture asking kids to write down free associations and not first having to go through the usual "Suppose nothing comes into my mind, I have no pencil, I lost my pad" business? At Forest everyone is leaking with creativity and competing like mad. The kids responded instantly to the phrase "scarlet snow" with all sorts of images; some close to the words like "maroon velvet chairs," "bloody battlefields," "Russia in winter," and "dead crows with broken beaks." Others were even further out, really imagining freely the way a patient might after six years of practice on the analyst's couch—which some of these kids are already well into.

I, in response to such responsiveness, got hold of an imagist poem, a real one labeled such in any good standard book, The Lady, *by Amy Lowell. "What kind of figure do you see?" I asked, and lo and behold, the kids zeroed out. "I wasn't really listening. I can't concentrate when someone reads."*

"How about the rest of you?"

Stillness, silence. Could it be?

"All right," I said. "I'll tell you what came into my mind." Before I finished with my exquisite, slightly altered, teacherly

image, Kirk blurted out, "That's just your interpretation, Ellen."

"You're damned right," I answered.

"Well," he went on, "I have my own picture and it's a man, not a woman."

"But, Kirk, listen to what the poem says," and I went on reading the poem. But Kirk still insisted that sun-flooded silks, perfumed souls, and smoldering roses—fallen, no less— add up to a man. Although the kids here are encouraged to think of the sexes as interchangeable, there's another explanation to account for why Kirk sees a lady as a man.

A child-centered school does get rid of repressions, but at the expense of any respect for authority. As long as something comes from within, it's of value because it has been created, even if it goes against the actual intent of the author, his interpreter (me), or anyone else, for that matter. That created something doesn't have to have any relation to the subject at hand for Kirk—admittedly an extreme case—to throw it out for grabs. He really has no idea that there are ideas that exist outside himself!

The kids even had a hard time listening to each others' creations. Only their own were of interest, and it was impossible for them to put together a poem based on all the individual images, because no single line would then stand out for attention.

Tant pis for poetry, but not for me because this whole experience has revived my missionary spirit, missing since the days at Andrews. But this time I'm not crusading to make prissy little school girls socially conscious; this time it's the more modest conversion of just having these kids acknowledge something outside of themselves. (Like a teacher!) Perhaps standard poetry isn't the way, but I'm reluctant to throw away creativity. So I decided to try something that's worked before: connecting the study of imagery to the surest world the kids know—TV. I plunged right into "onion pearls" and other delicious ads for peas, and kept things moving with the knights in shining armor who crash through kitchens to clean up dishes.

The kids were very helpful; they know the precise product the knight is pushing, so I could concentrate on the sneaky use of symbols. Many of the parents work in advertising, so it's a familiar thing. But what I care about now is that the kids are getting so excited they want to create their own ads. "And we can use them in the Forest Bulletin," they pointed out, and then I had it—the new job for the twelves, one with meaning, as Nellie would say. For the remainder of the afternoon we worked on ads and symbolism and imagery and saw how easy it is to manipulate the way people think if you have the right symbol and know how to use it. The kids ate this up too because it involves the whole notion of power. In a burst of excitement they asked if we could continue tomorrow; some said they were going to look through magazines to find good examples; others were going to make up their own.

Overflowing with my success, I stopped by to tell Nellie about the new project. Then I waited for her response.

Nothing. So I decided to do a little advertising myself. "Look, it has everything," I said. "It involves the energies of the kids. They actually initiated it, and it also can be tied up with the work project. They're learning about poetry and psychology," I stated as a side benefit. Nellie slowly gave out a grin.

"All that you say may be true, Ellen, but advertising is one of the greatest forces of corruption in our society. Were it not for advertising we wouldn't be buying all sorts of surplus goods we don't need which ruin our lives and make us unnecessarily acquisitive. Just think: if we didn't have such a selection at the supermarket, we might be tempted to grow our own vegetables. Advertising is something to be avoided, Ellen. I don't think it should be associated with poetry or, for that matter, talked about at all. And although I hate to lay down don'ts, I think I'll have to ask you to discontinue the project."

Can you believe that, Canelli? I regained my composure and fought back my tears.

"Perk up, Ellen, you'll come upon another idea. Or rather, the twelves will help you to discover one, as they have today."

"But, big magnanimous bigot of the modern world," I wanted to ask (but pride prevented me), "what do I do with these little monsters who have been walking in and out, bored beyond boredom, who today for the first time sat down and stayed?"

"After all, Ellen, the school is not here to serve your needs. Feeling uncomfortable and rejected in the beginning is something you must learn to live with." (I did admit today was the first time the kids seemed interested in class.) "Surely you don't want to use such feeling as a basis for a teaching program."

"Please, Nellie, it's been a hard day. Don't lecture to me like this."

"That's what I like to see, Ellen, some fight. Don't get defeated too fast. Go home, forget about all this, and come back tomorrow set to start over again." Undecided about starting all over again, I left.

———◆◆◆◆———

"Wait until you see my ad, Ellen, it's really the end."

"Yeah, show it to her, Kirk."

"Hold everything, Michael. We can't continue to work on ads. We have to think up another project instead."

"What do you mean?"

"Sit down, Kirk. You heard me. I have reasons."

"Then I'm not going to do anything."

"Okay. But if you do nothing, you must leave the room."

"No, I feel like staying. I'm just not going to do a thing."

"You're doing something right now—wasting my time—and I'm ordering you to leave."

"Shit. You'll have to drag me out."

"Okay, Kirk, let's go."

"Hey, Michael, look! She's really dragging him out! I wonder if he'll come back. No one ever laid a hand on Kirk before."

"He'll come back anyway, I bet."

"No, he won't, Jonathan. I'm locking the door."

"Look what he's doing now, Ellen."

"It's just amazing to see how one person can control a group of fifteen for such a long time. He'll do anything to get attention. I'm sure he *is* standing on his head and sticking out his tongue. But why do you let him dominate you that way?"

"You don't understand, Ellen. Kirk's very disturbed underneath."

"He's disturbed right on *top* too. I know he is, you know he is, *he* knows he is. But lots of us are disturbed without going around inflicting our disturbances on others all the time."

"But don't you think Kirk's funny?"

"Funny and fantastically charming. If he weren't, you wouldn't put up with his antics. You see—now that he's out, he wants to come in because out there he has no audience."

"I think we should let him in, Ellen. He really has no friends."

"What do you mean? He has all of you."

"But we're like his family."

"We're all he has."

"How many of you want him back in the room? Let's see. There are six hands raised. How many don't? Five? What about you three?"

"We don't want to vote."

"Okay, open the door, Michael, and tell him to come back in."

"I know you've been talking about me behind my back, Ellen. Don't deny it."

"I won't. What's more, I'll tell you everything I said. Of course, it's nothing new to you since you were the first person to clue me into these things."

"What things?"

"Your massive need for attention and the way you manage

to manipulate the rest of the class by always putting yourself into the center of the conversation. While you were out I asked the class why they allow you to do this."

"So, I'm a washout, a fadeout, a pretty punk who needs love more than a puppy dog. I know it. Thats' my tragedy. Not even my shrink can help me."

"You've told me that already, Kirk. In the first five minutes we met, in fact."

"I can't help it. My parents never loved me enough, and no psychiatrist can undo that. You know who understands me best? Taxicab drivers. They're the only ones. Much, much kinder than the best shrink."

"And less expensive, hey?"

"What do I care about money, Michael? You can really ride around for a long time, and if you get a good one, he'll listen to every word while he drives his cab."

"All right, Kirk, but now the problem is that we all want to participate in the class, and that doesn't seem possible with you around."

"You're all participating in my problems, aren't you?"

"I don't want to learn about your problems. Not here anyway."

"At least you're honest, Ellen. You're not a phony. I mean I can't stand people who pretend to be interested in me and really aren't."

"There you go again, dragging the subject back to you. Why don't you challenge yourself and see if you can withhold talk about yourself. You can even *think* about yourself as long as you keep your thoughts inside. Try it just once!"

"Why?"

"Oh, as a gift to me."

"Okay, but only as a gift, because I usually don't do things like that."

"No more, Kirk. It starts now. Where was I? Let's see; you kids have told me you don't want to study Greece, and I've told you that we can't study advertisements. How about talking about what's going on around us today?"

"You mean like social problems?"

"I guess you could call it that."

"Let's not do that, Ellen. It's a waste. I mean, sooner or later everyone sells out. Like our parents."

"Yeah, Mike, if they didn't we could never afford it here."

"Don't you have scholarships at Forest?"

"Not too many."

"Is that why there aren't any Negroes here?"

"No. That's because Nellie says its phony to go out looking for minority children. She wants only those who want to come. She's not going out looking for anyone, she says."

"What do you thing about that, Lisa?"

"I think she's right because Negro kids can't really afford to come here."

"There are some wealthy Negroes."

"I know because of my father—I mean my stepfather. But they don't like schools like this. They go to more regular kinds of schools."

"Only oddballs or beatniks or nuts like me come here."

"Hush, Kirk."

"You know where I want to go, Ellen? On a freedom ride down South."

"Leon, you'd get murdered. I mean they really rough up the people from up North. You have to know how to fight. I saw people getting beaten up by the police on TV."

"I don't blame the Southerners. I mean, they feel it's their land, and why should people come from somewhere else and tell them what to do when they've been doing things their own way for a long time?"

"It's worse up here, Nina, because they don't let Negroes into restaurants or country clubs."

"I saw a taxicab driver who passed a Negro by who was trying to hail a cab."

"I bet he picked you up, Kirk. How come you didn't ask him why he passed by the Negro?"

"I did, Nina. And he gave me a very good reason. He told me he had nothing against Negroes, but that he didnt' like to drive into bad neighborhoods. And once this cabby got cheated. The passenger said, 'Wait a minute while I go up to get the fare.' And then he never came back. And you know what? The cabby told me he felt lucky that he was only robbed instead of stabbed."

"But it's not fair."

"Oh, Leon, you and fairness! The world's not fair, don't you know that? Otherwise you wouldn't get picked on all the time."

"This whole thing is a complicated problem. I don't think there's a simple solution. Why don't you all think about it some more, and we'll continue the discussion tomorrow."

"Why cant' we stay after school today and continue talk-ing?"

"Because I'm busy this afternoon. How's tomorrow afternoon? I'm free then."

"Tomorrow afternoon stinks, but we have no choice."

"Right, Kirk."

Tues.

Where, Canelli, did we last leave off, in the jungle of aging progressive ideologies? Well, I'm back again. I am not going to allow Forest to turn an Andrews radical into the voice of conservatism. With one night's sleep tucked under the bags of my eyes, I returned, lighter and stronger, armed with a strategy—exploitation.

Yup, I'll exploit the lack of curriculum, teach whatever I feel like teaching. With advertising forbidden, I moved onto less corrupt topics like current affairs. The advertising project, short lived as it was, convinced me that the kids do want to learn, but that 12-year-olds don't have to have intellectual pursuits concealed by work-play. Nor do I have to pretend that adults learn more from children than the reverse. I decided I'm going to act like a teacher and take charge when need be.

Actually it's not all that daring to assert authority here. I'm convinced that the only reason the Forest teachers can denounce it is because they are such forceful and overwhelming personalities. Their appearance alone is enough to cow a child whose mother is always running around in pigtails and poncho when she isn't wearing long patio pajamas.

My first test of authority came when Kirk confronted me. Kirk, the beautiful precocious miniature male narcissist, mature beyond size in the uses of seduction by confession.

Now when Kirk started to fuss I simply walked over and grabbed his delicate arm and dragged him out as he went limp. One unequivocal advantage of private schools over public is that teachers are not prevented by law from abusing children! The class was shocked by my toughness, but Kirk enjoyed it because it made him look like a martyr, which is appealing to sensitive souls.

According to Nellie, Kirk's family does not care about him, which is why all the other kids are so kind to him. That plus the fact that he invites them to his country home, where they trot around in go-carts and the caretakers are so kind. All the poor little rich boy stuff that we used to read about but now can know about directly. Nellie says the parents lead a terribly indulgent life while Kirk does what he pleases.

Forest legend has it that Kirk arrives at seven in the morning. When the janitor wakes up he sees Kirk talking to stray cats, people, anyone passing by in the early dawn. (Echoes of Salinger?) The poor child, says Nellie, has been kicked out of three prep schools. And although the parents are ashamed that their son attends a progressive school like ours (thinks we're all a bunch of left-wing nuts), the truth is that we're the only school willing to accept Kirk and keep him. And, I might add, Kirk knows this, for he is one of the most perceptive youngsters I've ever met. Kirk knows we aren't afraid of disruptive children here. Indeed, he does! As a matter of fact, our whole aim is to encourage *disruptions in children, outbursts of natural energies that the rest of society is always trying to stifle.*

Although I cannot in any honesty report that I am reform-

ing anyone, I'm trying to prevent cynicism from seeping in too early and the kids from dropping out of society—which is the great danger with children like this.

———— ◄◄◆►► ————

The kids returned filled with ideas about reforming society and all sorts of idealistic schemes for changing the order of the universe. I was overjoyed again and felt certain that Nellie would share my enthusiasm this time. It was late when I left the school because I had stayed to talk with the kids, but Nellie was still in her office.

"Can you come in?" she said as I passed by. Jo was sitting next to Nellie, whose hands were clasped around her elbows. Both looked sternly at me.

"I want you to know, Ellen," said Jo, "that it is *I* who overheard the discussion going on in your room. I don't believe in spying or anything like that. I just happened to overhear what was being said, and that is how Nellie found out about it. I thought you ought to know that no one was intentionally checking up on you."

"As far as *I* could hear, we were talking about current events."

Now Nellie took over. "That's precisely it," she said. "I thought that my explanation yesterday would suffice. We believe, Ellen, that childhood is a beautiful time, and we don't think it should be ruined by burdening children with problems they can't solve."

I looked blankly at the two of them. "How *do* you teach children a sense of responsibility?"

"We have our ways. You yourself have seen how each twelve

is in charge of a four during some part of the day. That's a responsibility a 12-year-old can handle and won't abandon in frustration. We want to preserve the innocent quality of child-hood. It lasts for a short enough time without any acceleration on our parts. Left on their own, most children are wiser and kinder than adults. We can learn a lot from children when adult ways of thinking are not imposed on them at too early an age."

"But they seemed to enjoy the discussion. They were stimu-lated by it. Even Kirk participated in a way that was unusual for him. I mean he didn't just talk about himself."

"Perhaps so. But if they worry about Africa tonight, or Har-lem, what can they *do* about it but have nightmares?"

"I think there are things in the community they can do. And if they can't do anything about social conditions, they can learn about them."

"I know, in private schools it's very fashionable to get chil-dren involved in such activities, but we oppose them here. We don't believe in that kind of liberal phoniness. Most of the parents are very liberal and therefore the children will be too. We want to give them something they don't get at home, some respite from this century. That is why we stress Yard and Rhythms, activities that most city kids don't engage in."

Monday

Well, Canelli,

When I arrived this morning my first impression was that someone had died. Why else, I wondered, would every single child be seated quietly in his seat first thing in the morning, and Jo, Nellie, Annie and Dewey up front.

"*All right, Leon, why don't you let Ellen in on the whole thing?*"

"*Jo, don't make Leon confess like that.*"

"*Kirk, you keep quiet or get out.*"

"*Okay, but that's real dirty, Jo. I don't like it one bit.*"

"*There's no big secret hidden anymore,*" said Jo. "*Why don't we tell Ellen the facts? Leon brought in some marijuana and has been handing it out. It's as simple as that.*"

"*We ought to tell Leon—if he doesn't already know—that Forest could be closed down if the students started to peddle pot.*"

"*I'm glad you mentioned that, Annie. Ordinarily, we want everyone to feel free to do as he pleases here. I want you to think of Forest as a refuge or a sanctuary where we'll see to it that your safety is guaranteed. But you, in turn, cannot endanger us. There are some laws we are not free to violate merely because we would no longer be in business. You should all know that self-survival is the first consideration of even the most primitive society,*" quoth Nellie.

"*I think we ought to be frank about this,*" Dewey said. "*Only somebody who's desperate for friends tries to buy friendship by bribing others with forbidden things.*"

"*Leon didn't smoke any, Dewey,*" said Kirk, springing up from his seat.

"*All the more reason why Leon is to be condemned. Only a coward peddles something that he won't try himself.*"

"*Quit it, Dewey. Lay off Leon or I'm leaving.*"

"*Kirk, why do you take it upon yourself to defend Leon instead of letting Leon learn how to defend himself?*"

"*Look, Nellie, I know what it's like not to be wanted. I*

understand Leon. He had to bring in that stuff. He stinks in Yard, no one listens to him when he shows off all his information, and so what else can he do?"

"But that's weak and cowardly, Kirk."

"That's why I don't blame him. He is weak and cowardly, Dewey, and no one here respects him. Just like with me. Same old story all over again."

"Kirk, you don't understand that what upsets me as much as handing out the pot—free pot that Leon paid a pretty penny for, which he can hardly afford—is that he then dares to tell me the names of the people who smoked it. And you, Kirk, my dear, were one of them."

"I admit it. But don't you understand that the reason Leon did that was the same reason he handed out the pot in the first place? He thought it would make him popular, and when he saw it didn't, he had to get some revenge. Why can't you see that, Dewey?"

"Still, no one likes the guy who spills the beans. Can't you see that, Kirk?"

"Annie, if Leon used his brains for real life the way he uses them to solve problems on paper, he'd be a much healthier person. I know that from watching him in Rhythms."

"The question we must now face is, how are we going to prevent this from happening again here on the school grounds?"

Immediately the kids grasped the technicality of her argument. Nellie, they saw, was trying to squirm out of opposition to pot on the basis of location.

"Do you mind if we smoke it someplace else?"

Now Nellie was stuck. She hated to come out with a real

no; restrictions went against her ideology. "Well, that's a difficult distinction to make, because let's suppose you have some marijuana with you at home and have no intention of bringing it here, but just happen *to* forget *to remove it when you come to school, and some visitor is around who sees it."*

"How about if we keep it at home and never put it in our pockets, Nellie? Then that couldn't happen."

"Why are you arguing so strongly, Michael? According to Leon, you were hesitant to try it at first."

"Just at first. I did later."

"Come on, Michael, let us in on your secret pleasures," said Dewey. "I think it's selfish of you to keep them to yourself. I have never smoked pot, and I'm curious to know what I'm missing. Well, if you do not intend to talk up—if you, Michael Sims, have become shy all of a sudden—why, then, I have a good mind to take the confiscated stuff right to my own quarters and try it myself! And I'll report to you all whether it is worth all this bother."

Ah, the reasons repressed people give for trying to unre-press themselves! Always having to do with checking up on someone else's doing or seeing if any time and energy are being wasted. The old private school obsession—waste.

"That's it, Dewey. Three cheers, everyone."

"Hold on. I haven't finished. If I find anyone with mari-juana on school territory, I'll also take it on my own to pun-ish the person, and when I make up my mind to punish some-one I don't go back on my decision. Now is the last oppor-tunity for anyone who still has some to turn it in. Okay, I'm assuming that the rest of you are clean if I search you, which I just may decide to do in Rhythms later on. Ha, I knew I'd

get the sly ones who are still holding out. Come on, you fugitives, let's have it. Right into this envelope, fellas. And Lisa, you too. Now this should do it. You can all head to the gym where you'll cleanse your consciences with physical work."

Tuesday

At least now I have my class under control. No one walks out when I talk, and the kids even listen.

Are you wondering what potent drug I have handed out to still such free spirits and win pupils? The most potent of them all—sex. Vicariously, through talk, which so far has sufficed. It all came about naturally, the way sex should. One day I asked the class what they would like to learn.

Leon, still trying to redeem himself from the pot fiasco, shouted out, "Biology."

"Hey, Ellen," Rhea asked, "what's the rubber thing my mother says you have to wear once you become a woman?" So, good Catholic that I'm not, I proceeded to explain the contraceptive function of diaphragms.

"Do they hurt?" the girls asked, and I assured them that they do not. With pain out of the way, curiosity reared itself.

"How can a piece of rubber prevent creation?" they asked, as if that were more miraculous than creation itself—which I'd taken for granted all the kids knew until one girl screamed out in the midst of an explanation of the highest scientific order, "Ugh, Ellen, you mean that the 'slimy white stuff that comes out at night'" (quotation courtesy of Kirk) "goes inside me? That's horrible."

Now it was my turn for surprise. How come kids as sophisticated as these are so ignorant about sex? I couldn't believe it after all Dewey's talk about the experimentation that goes on in the "sex sessions" which she's convinced take place all the time. "What else do you think goes on in the bathrooms? Children are too young for constipation, so I think it's safe to say that if they don't come out after a few minutes they are having sex sessions. Which may be the reason why the kids leave the room so frequently."

But Dewey is not totally reliable about these things, since she is convinced that a kid is having a sex session when he rolls his spaghetti, disappears behind a library stack, or just sits quietly in his seat.

The other interesting thing besides their ignorance, is the kids' embarrassment. *Although physical freedom is stressed here, it is felt that in order to achieve it the distinction between boys and girls must be ignored. Girls are taught that they are as strong as boys and can do anything the boys can do, which seems to be true. The girls* do *climb the school fire escapes with as much ease as the boys bake bread. And of course they all dress the same way—in workmen's clothes which allow them to somersault over wooden planks just the way a longshoreman (the model for school dress) must do when he comes home after a day's work.*

The one sex distinction retained is that between the girls' and boys' bathrooms. Dewey is now trying to do away with it, but that's because *"you want to be able to peek at every-*one."

The best thing about sex is that I am teaching and the kids are learning. Even Kirk stays in the room, although he constantly interrupts to share his private sexual fantasies. The other thing that makes teaching these kids a pleasure is that they are so interested in themselves that they don't pry into my own personal life. The whole question of marriage is not connected with sex, which makes these kids genuinely different from the others I've known.

Sunday

Wouldn't you know, Canelli, that like all good primitive societies Forest has its rites of initiation? It all started casually enough with Nellie asking me on my last Friday whether I would join the group Saturday, that sacred night, at the "nest," the off-hours name for her apartment.

Rae was the first to greet me: "Come in, Ellen, I've been waiting for you." Things looked different. The atmosphere was subdued. Candles were burning; there was soft talk and some laughter, an open bottle of wine and one of Scotch. The most striking difference, though, was in the appearance of the women; maybe it was the dark lighting, but they didn't look like aging suffragettes tonight. Which meant they weren't in their plain shirts and straight skirts. Everyone was fully clothed and yet the setting was for seduction. Finally, I stopped being bored, curious, ironic, and decided to leave. (Rites of initiation which I flunked by default.) Rae insisted on accompanying me, and for the first time, we talked.

I learned a few things from Nellie related to the early history of the school—how its founder had been a big upstate girl who never lost her love for the country even after becoming one of the first female labor organizers, and how it was her experience with rotten schools that made her decide to go into teaching. But it was her experience with an eminent educator whose course she took around the turn of the century that inspired her to find her own school: he said that the first thing you do with little children when they arrive early in the morning is sit them down in a circle and sing them a song. A circle? Why impose order on free spirits? It is the children who should decide how they want to sit, if indeed they want to sit, early in the morning. The founder began to suspect that all education is a sneaky way of imposing restrictions on children who are otherwise free. And her suspicion was further confirmed when the eminent educator suggested that after the children sit in a circle, the teacher play some imaginative music so that the children could flutter around like butterflies. Now the founder could not contain her emotions.

"Children do not want to be butterflies," she said. "They want to be lions running and roaring as lions like to do."

"At Forest," Nellie told me with pride, "we have always let our children be lions and roar as much as they want." What I want to tell Nellie, but am telling you instead, is that children want to be lions and roar all day long, indeed. But there are others who want to be butterflies, and anyplace which forces all butterflies to roar like lions is not free.

Wednesday, the fifteenth of September

In New York City public schools, day-to-day teaching is known as per diem work. The only condition is that you have to be willing to teach in a slum area, but you do have the choice of slums.

Just keep your attendance book in order, and nobody will complain.

·⊰EPILOGUE⊱·

WHEN I FIRST started to consider writing this book, New York City was having the longest teachers' strike in the history of the public school system. Thank God, I thought, that my schools are private or else I might not have a subject. But as I continued to work, I began to wonder if any schools would exist, at least in the form I was describing, by the time I finished. All over the country new schools are cropping up—schools organized by students, schools where the community is the classroom, and schools where the distinction between student and teacher is disappearing. Not only are schools themselves changing enormously but the rate of change is staggering.

When I confided these dark thoughts to a friend—an alumnus of a boys' prep school, no less—he told me not to worry. "Private schools are different from public schools," he said. "They are very slow to change." Reassured by his words, I picked up the morning paper before resuming work. There on the front page was a story about two of the nations' oldest private schools, Choate and Rosemary Hall, teaming up, followed the next day by news of Vassar and Bennington going coed, and culminated on the third by a report that the headmaster at Horace Mann had agreed to let the boys decide for themselves how they should dress for class. I no longer felt reassured.

As the year advanced, I began to find comfort in those scarey little news items as I realized that precisely because private schools were beginning to recognize that they could not remain little worlds, private unto themselves, they would hold together and assure me of a subject.

Not that the kids who attend private schools are less rich and priviledged than they used to be; no, it's that being a preppie is no longer confined to traveling more and wearing better clothing. Not long ago it meant drunken college weekends, winter and spring vacations with one's roommates, but always accompanied by the expectation of a return to routine. The rich have eternally felt entitled to brief binges and flings; being a preppie today more often means being able to afford experimenting with new life styles.

Maybe one result of growing up in a scientific age is that experimentation is real; kids don't have the answers before they set out to explore the new. Nor do they know they will return to the world they leave when they take off for the junior year abroad which is more likely to be Appalachia or Harlem than Florence or Rome. Why, kids ask, should they let adulthood crush them down with the full weight of its burden of boredom? Are their parents happy or are they too busy devoting their lives to success to even wonder about happiness? Affluence has freed the young from financial ambition. (If you have any doubts about it just read the *Wall Street Journal* and *Fortune*. They can't afford to lie; too much money is at stake.)

.EPILOGUE.

Kids don't want to be individuals, not in the old sense. They want to be part of a group, to share, to belong to a community, live like a tribe, set up a commune. Private school kids want to lose their little private selves that everyone has cultivated for them—which is why the current search for identity so often lands in social involvement. (In a world where nothing is impossible, it becomes all the more insane that so much remains wrong.) Which is also why so many rich white kids carry on love affairs, either symbolically or actually, with a member of a minority group. It's the minorities who must form groups, who know best what loyalty and solidarity is all about.

Minority groups have pushed the notion of identity beyond the individual, which may also explain why individual therapy is losing its popularity and giving way to groups who "encounter" and "confront" each other—not only with their minds but with their bodies as well as in the "new" fusion of sound, body, and mind dating back only to the Golden Age of the Greeks! What appears like a picnic for Dionysis is not a mad sexual orgy but a total revolution of life style. Only those adults obsessed by sex *per se*—sex unrelated to politics, sex unrelated to art, sex unrelated to all that gives life drama, see youth as a new species out only for "animal pleasure." In other words, only dirty old men (which include headmistresses) see youth as dirty *young* men.

It's religion-oriented teachers and parochial schools in general who remain totally out of touch with the youth movement. They are concerned with preserving a way of life that rests on religious dogma—which rarely rests, in turn, on expansion of consciousness, expansion of experience into the new and unknown. The very notion of expansion is contradictory to the meaning of parochial—narrow and enclosed, if not entirely cloistered.

The traditional private schools which were once as parochial in their own way, may not wish to change but realize that if they are to continue, they must. And if change is not as slow as my dear ex-preppie thought or as fast as I feared, it *is* going on usually within the framework of the existing structure—which for most traditional private schools means that teachers still retain authority. And educationally, teachers still do. That is, most students acknowledge that teachers know more than they do about English, Botany, or Calculus. The area where faculty authority is being questioned is in *moral* matters. Teachers today who command the greatest respect aren't those who try to direct the lives of their students— they're the ones who refrain from judging how an individual lives while remaining morally committed. At the core of this moral commitment is a certain kind of honesty. Students are in desperate search of authenticity, which to them means the ability to express doubts—doubts about schools, about governments, about themselves. Old-fashioned teachers who still believe in a fixed order of the universe are considered unreliable, while those with a humility about judging others are considered strong. Students today believe that each individual has a right to decide what kind of life he will lead, even if it goes against all the teachings of traditional society. Have all the judges their parents consulted—the psychiatrists, the educators, the marriage counselors—helped?

Along with this suspension of judgment is an absolute,

even puritanical judgment about an individual's political and societal roles. Excuses and rationalizations for acts of injustice and indifference are considered just that—excuses, cover-ups, lies. Admitting you've lost is no longer a sign of cowardice and confession is a strength which may be the biggest revolution for the preppie, whose trademarks once were winning and keeping a stiff upper lip.

In contrast, progressive schools have never stressed winning and are ideologically opposed to competition, committed to change, progressive, community, physical expressiveness, crafts, and opposed to bigness, bureaucratic methods, and all the other ills of urban life.

The one problem with a progressive school is that in building rebellion right into its structure, what form can spontaneous student protest take? One thing students can do—and are doing—is dropping out of society altogether since any kind of protest seems stale and phony. And it is stale and phony if it's not of their own doing.

Educationally, the progressive school is more rebellious too, which at times encourages an anti-intellectualism rarely present in the traditional private school. On the other hand, progressive schools encourage creative children who are often ignored, if not outrightly stifled, in traditional schools. Their graduates are almost always recognizable by their appreciation of the dramatic, the creative, and the artistic.

In choosing a school for a child, I would offer this advice to parents who feel schools should act as some kind of compensation for a home atmosphere—more specifically, to parents who have brought their children up in what they consider too permissive a fashion and look for a highly structured school to balance things out. It's a myth that such balancing takes place. If any generalization holds, it is that children feel most comfortable in familiar environments. Children from permissive homes feel most at ease in permissive schools, just as children from structured homes seem to enjoy structure in the classroom. Schools may help to mold a child, but they shouldn't be expected to reshape him.

Another myth is that children in progressive schools are more disturbed, often because the divorce rate is higher among the parents. On the basis of what I've seen, there is no simple correlation except that more divorced parents send their children to private schools of all sorts, because private schools spend more time with a child, which makes a parent more at ease.

And lastly, having written a book based on my teaching experiences, I won't avoid the inevitable question of where would *I* send my child to school? Unless my neighborhood had a public school which was a real community school, chances are I'd send my child to private school. Yep, I believe private schools do a better job of educating a person and give him a more enlightened world perspective. Private school classes are smaller; teachers are usually better educated and more diverse (once again: they, like their students, can afford to be), and private schools rarely roll out the bureaucratic machinery so crushing to growth. The particular school I would choose would suit my particular values—a school somewhere between Andrews and Forest—one both progressive and diverse. For then I would know that should my progeny choose to concentrate on Arabic and flute, he would also learn how to read and write English, solve problems in science and math, and even learn something about computers if he elected to become part of contemporary life. But most comforting of all would be the knowledge that should my child turn out to be sensitive and sedate, he could stroll freely through life without worrying about why he chose not to romp and gambol.

DATE DUE		
NOV 16 '70	OCT 23 1973	
NOV 30 '70	NOV 27 1973	
FEB 4	JAN 1 3 75	
FEB 15 7	JUN 8 '76	
MAR 1 8 7	NOV 10 7	
APR 6 '7	APR 15 '82	
NOV 1 9 7	OCT 4	
JAN 3	JAN 2 8 '83	
FEB 17 72	AUG 5 '8	
MAR 3 0	NOV 22 '85	
OCT 4 '7		
APR 1 8 1973		